Making Se
of the
Old Testament

3 Crucial Questions

Grant R. Osborne and Richard J. Jones, Jr., editors

3 Crucial Questions about Jesus
  Murray J. Harris
3 Crucial Questions about the Bible
  Grant R. Osborne
3 Crucial Questions about the Holy Spirit
  Craig S. Keener
3 Crucial Questions about Spiritual Warfare
  Clinton E. Arnold
3 Crucial Questions about the Last Days
  Daniel J. Lewis
Making Sense of the Old Testament: 3 Crucial Questions
  Tremper Longman III
3 Crucial Questions about Women (forthcoming)
  Linda L. Belleville
3 Crucial Questions about Black Theology (forthcoming)
  Bruce J. Fields
3 Crucial Questions about the Trinity (forthcoming)
  Millard J. Erickson
3 Crucial Questions about Salvation (forthcoming)
  Richard J. Jones, Jr.
3 Crucial Questions about Moral Reasoning (forthcoming)
  Kevin J. Vanhoozer
3 Crucial Questions about Racial Reconciliation (forthcoming)
  Raleigh B. Washington

Other Books by Tremper Longman III

Bold Love (with Dan Allender)
Bold Purpose (with Dan Allender)
The Book of Ecclesiastes
A Complete Literary Guide to the Bible (co-editor with Leland Ryken)
God Is a Warrior (with Daniel G. Reid)
How to Read the Psalms
Intimate Allies (with Dan Allender)
An Introduction to the Old Testament (with Raymond B. Dillard)
Old Testament Commentary Survey, 2d ed.
Reading the Bible with Heart and Mind

Making Sense
of the
Old Testament

3 Crucial Questions

Tremper Longman III

Baker Academic
Grand Rapids, Michigan

© 1998 by Tremper Longman III

Published by Baker Academic
a division of Baker Publishing Group
P.O. Box 6287, Grand Rapids, MI 49516-6287
www.bakeracademic.com

Seventh printing, December 2006

Printed in the United States of America

Library of Congress Cataloging-in-Publication Data
Longman, Tremper.
      Making sense of the Old Testament: 3 crucial questions / Tremper Longman.
          p.   cm. — (3 crucial questions)
      Includes bibliographical references and indexes.
      ISBN 10: 0-8010-5828-7 (pbk.)
      ISBN 978-0-8010-5828-8 (pbk.)
          1. Bible. O.T.—Criticism, interpretation, etc. 2. Bible. O.T.—Theology. I. Title.
      II. Series.
      BS1171.2.L66   1999
      221.6—dc21   98-30481

Unless otherwise indicated, all Scripture quotations are taken from the Holy Bible, New Living Translation, copyright © 1996. Used by permission of Tyndale House Publishers, Inc., Wheaton, Illinois 60189. All rights reserved. Other translations cited include the King James Version (KJV) and the New International Version (NIV).

To my son
Timothy Scheetz Longman
on heading off to college in 1998—
it is hard on your mother and me
as you strike out on your own,
but exciting to see how you have matured
physically, mentally, and spiritually

Contents

Editors' Preface

The books in the 3 Crucial Questions series are the published form of the 3 Crucial Questions Seminars, which are sponsored by Bridge Ministries of Detroit, Michigan. The seminars and books are designed to greatly enhance your Christian walk. The following comments will help you appreciate the unique features of the book series.

The 3 Crucial Questions series is based on two fundamental observations. First, there are crucial questions related to the Christian faith for which imperfect Christians seem to have no final answers. Christians living in eternal glory may know fully even as they are known by God, but now we know only in part (1 Cor. 13:12). Therefore, we must ever return to such questions with the prayer that God the Holy Spirit will continue to lead us nearer to "the truth, the whole truth, and nothing but the truth." While recognizing their own frailty, the authors contributing to this series pray that they are thus led.

Second, each Christian generation partly affirms its solidarity with the Christian past by reaffirming "the faith which was once delivered unto the saints" (Jude 3 KJV). Such an affirmation is usually attempted by religious scholars who are notorious for talking only to themselves or by nonexperts whose grasp of the faith lacks depth of insight. Both situations are unfortunate, but we feel that our team of contributing authors is well prepared to avoid them. Each author is a competent Christian scholar able to share tremendous learning in down-to-earth language both laity and experts can appreciate. In a word, you have in hand a book that is part of a rare series, one that is neither pedantic nor pediatric.

The topics addressed in the series have been chosen for their timelessness, interest level, and importance to Christians everywhere. And the contributing authors are committed to discussing them in a manner that promotes Christian unity. Thus, they discuss not only areas of disagreement among Christians but significant areas of agreement as well. Seeking peace and pursuing it as the Bible commands (1 Peter 3:11), they stress common ground on which Christians with different views may meet for wholesome dialogue and reconciliation.

The books in the series consist not merely of printed words; they consist of words to live by. Their pages are filled not only with good information but with sound instruction in successful Christian living. For study is truly Christian only when, in addition to helping us understand our faith, it helps us to live our faith. We pray therefore that you will allow God to use the 3 Crucial Questions series to augment your growth in the grace and knowledge of our Lord and Savior Jesus Christ.

Grant R. Osborne
Richard J. Jones, Jr.

Author's Preface

The Old Testament, the Word of God written before the coming of Christ, constitutes over three-quarters of the Bible. However, if we are honest with ourselves, we spend far less time reading and studying the Old Testament than we do the New. Indeed, many Christians spend no time in the Old Testament.

Even as an Old Testament professor, I can appreciate the attraction of the New Testament. After all, the New Testament is the fulfilment of the Old. Why spend an inordinate amount of time with the shadow when the reality has already come? The New Testament speaks more directly to us because its authors tell us about Jesus Christ.

Not only is the Old Testament difficult to appreciate, it is also difficult to understand. We are distanced from the Old Testament not only by its position in redemptive history (we live in the period after Christ; the Old Testament comes from the time before Christ), but also by time and culture. It is simply a hard book for us to interpret and appropriate to our daily lives.

My argument in this volume is that it is vitally important for us to work at our appreciation and understanding of the Old Testament. Jesus himself told us that the Old Testament remained crucial even after his fulfilment of it (Matt. 5:17–20). Indeed, many passages and images of the New Testament are virtually impossible to understand without recourse to their Old Testament background. This is particularly true of books like Matthew, Hebrews, and Revelation, but to a lesser extent it is also true of the whole New Testament.

As we study the Old Testament, we will also be surprised by a fundamental insight into its radical importance for all Christians: at the center of the Old Testament stands Jesus Christ. Augustine was right when he wrote his famous words: "The New Testament is in the Old concealed; the Old Testament is in the New revealed."

It is my great hope that this book will help revive in the reader a sense of the importance of the Old Testament for Christian faith and practice. I also pray that my words will give help to those who struggle with the proper interpretation of the oldest portions of God's written revelation to his human creatures.

Finally, I would like to thank Grant Osborne and Richard Jones for the opportunity to contribute this volume to the 3 Crucial Questions series. I appreciate their editorial guidance. I would also like to thank the staff at Baker Book House for their willingness to put my book in print.

What Are the Keys to Understanding the Old Testament?

An Overview of Old Testament Study: Attractions and Obstacles

The ~~Attractions~~ of the Old Testament

1. ~~GRIPPING STORIES~~

In my travels and correspondence, I see that Christians have an increasing interest in the Old Testament. While, in my opinion, we still don't spend enough time studying and reflecting on God's revelation before the coming of Jesus, I am extremely excited to observe that people are turning to the Hebrew Bible to learn more about God and more about a godly life.

A variety of factors have been attracting Christians to the Old Testament lately. Prominent among them are its gripping stories. We love stories. A good story can hold our attention for hours.

We will stay rooted in a chair as we listen to someone tell a story or as we read a good book.[1]

The Old Testament is a repository of varied stories about the most fascinating people. As we begin in Genesis, we encounter the story of Abraham's physical journey from Ur of the Chaldees to the Promised Land and of his developing relationship with God. We read about Joseph, cast into a pit by his brothers, rising to a position of great prominence in Egypt, and saving his family, the people of God, from death by starvation. Next comes Exodus with its tales of Moses and the burning bush, the ten plagues, and the crossing of the Red Sea. The list goes on and on: Joshua and Jericho; Samson and Delilah; David and Goliath; Elijah and Elisha; Ezra and Nehemiah. These stories stimulate our imaginations and evoke deep emotions.

As we read Old Testament stories, we encounter not only spellbinding plots, but vivid characters. We do not get modern-style biographies in the Bible, but we do find character portraits. We have an intuitive understanding that these character portraits are given to us to help us navigate life. Paul in fact explicitly tells us that that is their purpose. In 1 Corinthians 10:1–11 he recalls to mind some significant events from Old Testament history and then offers a generalization: "These events happened as a warning to us, so that we would not crave evil things as [our ancestors] did or worship idols as some of them did" (vv. 6–7). Among the more potent warnings is the account of the disastrous consequences of Solomon's marriages to foreign wives (1 Kings). His transformation from the wisest of all kings to a fool who brings down the kingdom is a solemn caution against godless entanglements.

In addition to warnings, the Old Testament narratives present us with ideals to emulate. Daniel and his three friends serve as an extraordinary example of faith during persecution. When cast into the furnace, the three friends trusted God even though they knew they might be roasted alive. Listen to their testimony to Nebuchadnezzar: "We do not need to defend ourselves before you. If we are thrown into the blazing furnace, the God whom we serve is able to save us. He will rescue us from your power, Your Majesty. But even if he doesn't, Your Majesty can be sure that we will never serve your gods or worship the gold statue you have set up" (Dan. 3:16–18). These Old Testament stories have additional punch because they are true. We can learn much from fiction, but our attention is riveted by historical characters and events that actually happened.

2. Heart-Wrenching Poems

But there is more to the Old Testament than stories. A good portion of the Old Testament is poetic.[2] Poetry in ancient Hebrew, as in most other literary traditions, is compressed language, saying a lot in only a few words. Poetry is particularly appealing because it so obviously addresses us as whole people. It is not interested just in informing our intellects, but in evoking our emotions, stimulating our imaginations, and influencing our wills.

The Psalms have been a perpetual favorite among Christians. Throughout church history the Psalms have been used as sources for hymns, as encouragements to prayer life, and as corporate responsive readings. These poems, the expressions of their authors' intense emotions, never make concrete (except perhaps in their titles) the particular situation that gave rise to their joy or sorrow. The historical nonspecificity of the Psalms renders them an appropriate vehicle for community worship. In other words, later worshipers can appropriate the Psalms for their own prayers and mold the words to fit their own situation. We in effect become the "I" of the psalm.

John Calvin observed that as we pray or sing a psalm, that psalm serves as a mirror of our soul. "What various and resplendent riches are contained in this treasure, it were difficult to find words to describe. . . . I have been wont to call this book, not inappropriately, an anatomy of all parts of the soul; for there is not an emotion of which anyone can be conscious that is not here represented as in a mirror."[3] Just as a physical mirror reflects our physical appearance, the Psalms afford us a look into our soul. If we feel at one with the psalmist as he expresses his love for God, then we know that our relationship with God is strong. On the other hand, we may find that Psalm 130, which begins, "From the depths of despair, O LORD, I call for your help," better expresses what we feel. The latter is typical of the lament psalms, which reflect disorientation in relationship with the Lord. Such psalms, with only one exception (Ps. 88), point us back to God by concluding with either an expression of confidence in him or a hymn of praise.

3. IMAGES OF GOD

Christians are also drawn to the Old Testament because we encounter God in its pages. God reveals himself not only to his Old Testament people, but to us who read these accounts millennia later. The first two chapters of the Bible describe God as Creator of the cosmos and the source of human life. After the fall in Genesis 3, God appears in various forms to his chosen people to rescue them from distress, protect them from danger, and inform them of his will. To Abraham he appears as a flaming torch in a smoking pot (Gen. 15:17); to Moses he shows his back (Exod. 33:12–23); to the Israelites in the wilderness God makes his presence known through a pillar of fire and a cloud of smoke. These and many other appearances (theophanies) confront the reader with a God of mystery who reveals himself only partially (though truly) to his people.[4]

God also chooses to reveal himself in the Old Testament through metaphor, which serves the same purpose of preserving the mystery of God. Through imagery God shows himself to his people, while also veiling himself. It is of the nature of metaphor to communicate truly but not precisely. In what way is God like a father? a warrior? a shepherd? a husband?

Note that most of the metaphors for God that we encounter in the Old Testament are relationship metaphors. God's fatherhood presupposes our sonship. God as a warrior implies that we are soldiers in his army. Since relationship is so crucial to our human experience, we find ourselves drawn to these Old Testament metaphors to understand ourselves.

4. Guidance for Life

Along the same line, Christians find themselves attracted to the Old Testament in the hope that we might there gain insight into how to navigate life. This expectation accounts for the rise of interest in the law and wisdom literature, particularly the Book of Proverbs, among Christians. We hope to find principles for living that transcend the ancient world to shape our attitudes and behavior today. Some even feel that the Old Testament goes beyond individual guidance to provide a blueprint for society, the basis for a contemporary legal code for a nation that wants to please God.

5. Background to the New Testament

The more time one spends in the New Testament, the more one realizes how much of it flows from the Old. That one cannot really understand the New Testament without being steeped in the Old is an inescapable conclusion.

Why did Jesus have to die? What does Paul mean when he says that Jesus was the second Adam (Rom. 5:12–21)? What is the significance of Jesus' dying just before the Jewish festival of Passover? Why is there so much warfare imagery in the Book of Revelation? Finding the answers to such questions depends in large measure on a thoroughgoing acquaintance with the Old Testament.

Obstacles to Understanding the Old Testament

For a host of reasons, then, Christians find themselves reading and studying the Old Testament with eagerness. Both the narratives and the poetry of the Old Testament not only are riveting, but have the potential to transform our lives. They prepare the way for the coming of the Savior, Jesus Christ.

However, we must also admit that the church's interest in the Old Testament is highly selective. Christians struggle with the Old Testament because they ~~find large parts of it hard to under~~ ~~stand and of doubtful relevance~~ to their lives. It is ever so difficult to discipline ourselves to read it regularly. Ministers often avoid preaching from the Old Testament, concentrating on the more obviously relevant New Testament.

Even when we do make an effort to read the Old Testament, we are often baffled concerning its meaning. Why are we so passionless as we approach this large portion of God's Word? Why do we have such difficulty understanding its message and, perhaps most tellingly of all, its implications for our lives? I would suggest that the Christian community's ambivalence about the Old Testament is the result of more than our sin or our lack of intelligence. The reasons range from the mundane to the theological. Among the major causes of the feeling of distance from the Hebrew Bible are (1) its length, (2) its antiquity, (3) its foreignness, and (4) its place in the history of God's redemption. These four characteristics distance the reader at the beginning of the third millennium A.D. from the Word of God as it was revealed to his ancient people Israel before the coming of Jesus Christ.

1. ~~Length and Diversity~~

Long books are harder to read than short ones even when they are gripping novels. On a recent plane trip I overheard two Tom Clancy fans discussing his new book *Executive Orders.* They had read all the previous books recounting the exploits of their hero Jack Ryan. This latest volume was exciting enough, but it was over one thousand pages long, and in small print. They were struggling to get through it, but were determined to do so.

The Old Testament is a long book. Indeed, it constitutes 77 percent of the Bible. Not only is it hard to get through by virtue of its length, but the diversity of the writings also proves a formidable barrier. There are vast differences as one moves from Exodus to Leviticus, for example. The exciting story of the Israelites' release from Egyptian bondage is temporarily suspended for a technical discussion of sacrifices and priests. The story line of the Bible is often interrupted by laws, prophetic oracles, or lyric poetry. Thus it is a hard book to pick up and read from cover to cover. As a result, we find it difficult to get a sense of the whole. We read piecemeal, a psalm here and a chapter of prophecy there.

Let me take this opportunity to suggest that a frequent obstacle to reading large portions of the Old Testament, and the New for that matter, is the type of translation used by many Christians. Most translations of the Bible lack the compelling literary quality of the original languages. The literal, stilted, and sometimes archaic language which is used in the majority of English translations does not reflect the literary power of the original Hebrew stories and poems. The false notion that literal is more accurate, or that religious language must sound like Shakespearean English, has led to the production of English Bibles that are tedious to read. Please understand that I think literal versions like the New American Standard Bible and the New International Version have an important place in the church and in our study, as do high-style versions like the King James and the New Revised Standard. However, we must also acknowledge that they hinder sustained reading of large portions of Scripture.

2. Antiquity

In addition to being long, the Hebrew Bible is old, surely older than most books we read. True, the Old Testament is not the oldest writing we have. There are important religious and literary works from Egypt, Mesopotamia, and Canaan that predate the earliest portion of the Bible by centuries. Nonetheless, the Bible's antiquity provides a challenge to our understanding.

We sometimes forget how distanced we are from the Old Testament in terms of date. That is because many of us have grown up with a Bible in the home. Accordingly, we have a sense that it belongs to our time, our era, but that is misguided. The parts of the Old Testament closest to us in time come from no later than 400 B.C., nearly two-and-one-half millennia before we were born. These parts include postexilic works like 1 and 2 Chronicles, Ezra-Nehemiah, Haggai, Zechariah, and Malachi.

The oldest part of the Hebrew Bible is considerably older than the postexilic works. According to the Bible itself, Moses was the first individual to actually write down divine revelation for posterity. God had revealed himself before the time of Moses, but Moses was the first to inscripturate the revelation. Here arises the problem of when exactly to date Moses. Traditionally, most evangelical scholars have understood the Scriptures (passages like 1 Kings 6:1 provide guidance in this regard) to point to the fifteenth century B.C. for the time of Moses. However, the evidence can possibly be interpreted to indicate a period of time some two centuries later.[5] This is not important for our purposes; it is clear that the earliest portions of the Old Testament were written about one thousand years before the last parts.

Besides noting the antiquity of the Old Testament, we should be aware of the incredible length of time during which it came into existence. One thousand years is a long, long time. We must keep this vast space of time in mind as we read the different parts of the Old Testament.

3. Cultural Distance

Culture is difficult to define because its origins, motivations, and developments are highly complex phenomena. Art, music, relationship styles, attitudes toward strangers, clothing, forms of entertainment are all expressions of culture. Adding to the difficulty of definition is the fact that culture represents ~~the tastes not of individuals, but of society at large~~.

But even if we cannot define it precisely, we intuitively recognize differences in culture. We look at a picture from the sixties and chuckle at the hairstyles, the peace sign, the tie-dyed shirts, and the painted Volkswagen van. When we go to a museum of ancient artifacts, we are in for an even bigger shock. The art, literary expressions, relationships, and the practice of warfare strike us as bizarre. We may think to ourselves that if a time machine carried us back, the experience would be similar to encountering an alien from another planet.

Now the Bible was God's Word to a specific people. It was, like his Son, incarnational. God did not reveal himself in some type of transcultural way (which is in fact an inconceivable notion). ~~God's people lived in a specific culture, and he condescended to address them by using the conventions of their day.~~ We see this most clearly in the fact that he spoke to them in Hebrew. In order for us to hear God's Word today, we must bridge the cultural gap by translating the Hebrew into English. Such a task entails learning the linguistic conventions of Hebrew and working hard at rendering God's message in a modern idiom that reflects his ancient intention.

But it is not just language that is at issue here. Images, such as God as a shepherd (a royal image in the ancient Near East), drew from the contemporary experience of the ancient people of Old Testament times. Literary genres such as the treaty form of Deuteronomy arose in the ancient Near East and are not recognizable immediately today, because we do not use such forms.

All of this is to say that it is not only because of its length and antiquity that we find ourselves distanced from the Old Testament; we also must take into account that we are modern (or postmodern, if you prefer) African-Americans or white Americans reading ancient Semitic literature. We will encounter strange customs, literary forms, and institutions. We must take into account the cultural form of the text as we seek to understand and apply it to our own situations.

4. ~~POSITION IN THE HISTORY OF REDEMPTION~~

The fourth reason why we feel distanced from the Old Testament may be the most important. As Christians, our faith is appropriately ~~focused on Jesus Christ,~~ who died on the cross and was raised to save us from our sin. He is the one in whom we have the hope of eternal life. We learn about Jesus most clearly in the pages of the New Testament, not the Old. When we turn to the Old Testament, we find a religion which leaves us cold. We read of priests, sacrifice, festivals, circumcision, food laws, and the like. We read of bloody wars against Israel's enemies and encounter psalms beseeching God to take a foe's child and dash its head against a rock. When it comes to the all-important matter of redemption history and salvation, we find much of the ~~Old Testament irrelevant at best and offensive at worst.~~ Added to the obstacles of length, antiquity, and cultural distance, the practical result is that Christians don't spend as much time in the Old as they do in the New Testament.

Principles for Successful Interpretation

It is not surprising that we lack passion when we think of the Old Testament. Obstacles to understanding and easily applying it to our lives are abundant. In a word, we find ourselves at a distance from the Old Testament. Coming from the time before Jesus our Savior, it is old and culturally strange. Paradoxically, however, the first step that we must take to a healthy appropriation of the Old Testament is to fully embrace its distance from us. We will surely distort God's message to us if we read the Old Testament as if it had been written yesterday. We will surely misapply it to our lives and the communities in which we live if we don't take into account the discontinuity between the Israelites, who were the Old Testament people of God, and us Christians living at the beginning of the third millennium.

Acknowledging this distance leaves us with a gap between the Old Testament and ourselves. The task of the interpreter—and anyone who reads the Bible is an interpreter—is to bridge the gap between the ancient text and our modern situation in a way that does not infringe on the integrity of the original. What we are talking about here has the technical name of "hermeneutics." The first part of that word is taken from the Greek god Hermes, whose basic role was to deliver the messages of the other gods. In other words, the field of hermeneutics studies the nature of written communication.

The intention of the balance of this chapter is to suggest a basic hermeneutic for the study of the Old Testament. The principles we will enunciate are not rigid laws to be applied in the same way in every text; rather, they are principles to keep in mind in reading and studying the Old Testament.

Principle 1: Discover the Author's Intended Meaning

We begin with a clear statement of the fundamental goal of Old Testament study: discover the author's intended meaning. A clear understanding of this goal of interpretation is essential because of challenges presented to it in both popular thinking and scholarly writing.

Many times when I shared the gospel with a non-Christian relative or friend, I was met with the response, "Well, that's your interpretation." That statement seems so obvious and so non-contradictory that many people think it ends the conversation; more sadly, it counters the claims which the gospel is making on their lives. Let's unpack a bit what the statement means. Most people are vaguely aware that the interpretation of the Bible is somewhat debated. They know that there are different types of Christians; they also know that non-Christians adopt a totally different understanding of the text. Some take the Bible as historical, others as parabolic, still others as mythical, and a number as nonsensical. Further, while some people may agree that Genesis 1 reports a real space-time event, they will disagree as to whether the seven "days" of creation are twenty-four-hour periods of time, long geological periods, or even a term without any connection to chronology at all. The bottom line in such cases is that we have the option of taking the Bible any way we want. The way in which we have stated our first principle ("Discover the author's intended meaning"), however, indicates that when we declare, "The Bible says," we are not presenting our own views in the guise of an authoritative text, but the views of the prophets and apostles of old who spoke on God's behalf. This assertion, of course, does not answer the question of why we have different interpretations, but it does allow us a rejoinder: "Well, let's study the text together to see if what I just said is right or not."

Contemporary scholarship, of course, takes a much more sophisticated approach.[6] In a word, postmodern hermeneutics asserts that literary texts, the Bible included, have no determinate meaning. Since the days of the New Criticism of the 1940s and 1950s, to speak of the author's meaning has been considered a dead end. What has filled the void? ~~We have moved from the opinion that meaning resides in the text or in the reader to the idea that there is no meaning~~.

David J. A. Clines is the most influential recent writer in this area.[7] Making explicit the position of many other contemporary critics, Clines assumes and states that the interplay of the numerous authors, the biblical text, and its readers through the years prohibits our speaking of "the meaning" of any particular text. He then blatantly says that we are free to interpret the text any way that we choose.

So what determines the direction of Clines's own interpretations? Advocating what he calls "bespoke criticism," he cites the analogy of a tailor.[8] We go to a tailor with material and ask him to make a suit. He then cuts the cloth to meet our specifications because we pay him to do so. Now the biblical text is like the material. Clines can cut the cloth into a variety of shapes, but he chooses the way that his paying customers request. Thus, if he preaches in an Anglican church, he will shape the text one way. If he is speaking to a group of feminists, he will cut it another way. If he speaks to a vegetarian group, he will interpret the text in yet a different way.[9]

Now Clines's approach may strike the reader as absurd. Actually, it is not so much absurd as pitiful. It is a legitimate route for anyone with the basic presupposition that the Bible has no determinate meaning. But why would such a person continue to devote his life to the biblical text? (In a recent review I suggest that an even older and less respectable profession where people sell their wares to paying customers might be a more suitable analogy.)

In spite of the flaws in Clines's approach, we must admit that he and other cynics take their starting point from some real and profound problems with the position that we are arguing for here, so we must continue our discussion. We must defend our position that the meaning of a text resides in the author's intention.

The first issue with which we must grapple is the fact that we are not always certain of the identity of the human author of a biblical book. I do not even have in mind here hotly contested books like the Pentateuch, where Moses' role is debated, or the question whether Solomon wrote all, part, or none of the Song of Songs and Ecclesiastes. I am thinking of the numerous anonymous books of the Old Testament. A partial list would include Joshua, Judges, Ruth, 1 and 2 Samuel, 1 and 2 Kings, 1 and 2 Chronicles, many of the Psalms, and parts of Proverbs. We don't know the authors of these books; indeed, we are uncertain of the time period when some of them were written.

A closely related issue has to do with the number of authors of certain biblical texts. Some Old Testament books show fairly clear signs of later editorial activity, which even the most conservative scholars admit. In the Pentateuch we speak of post-Mosaica, that is, passages written after Moses' death (most strikingly the account of his death in Deut. 34), and a-Mosaica, passages that sound awkward in Moses' mouth (e.g., Num. 12:3). Further, the history books were probably written over a long period of time.

These two issues raise the question of what it means to ground the text's meaning in the intention of an author (or authors) whose name(s) we don't know and whose work we can't date with any level of certainty. But there are problems even in the case of those biblical books whose author we can identify. The issue here is that we have no independent access to any of the authors of the biblical account. How, then, can we confirm our interpretation of a passage through an appeal to its author? We can't interview Moses, David, or Nahum to ask him what he meant by his writings. We can't take the prophet Isaiah aside to inquire, "Whom did you have in mind when you spoke of the Suffering Servant in chapter 53? Were you thinking exclusively of a coming Messiah, or did you also have in mind Israel as a corporate entity?" An added difficulty is that we possess only one writing of most of the authors of the Old Testament, so we can't appeal to their other writings to get a better understanding, an approach we can take with a prolific author like Paul (though this brings its own problems).

A fourth issue concerns the relationship between the human author and the divine Author. This is an issue that arises only within a hermeneutic that takes seriously the Bible's own claim of ultimate divine authorship.[10] A biblical passage that raises the issue of the relationship between the human author and divine Author most dramatically is 2 Peter 1:20–21: "Above all, you must understand that no prophecy in Scripture ever came from the prophets themselves or because they wanted to prophesy. It was the Holy Spirit who moved the prophets to speak from God." This passage makes it clear that there is an inspiring force behind the writings of Moses, David, Jeremiah, Paul, Peter, and the others—God himself. So while it is certainly correct to call the ~~human beings whom God used to write his revelation authors,~~ ~~we must also speak of the ultimate Author, who is God himself.~~ Our concern here is what we mean when we say that the goal of our interpretation is the author's meaning. When we interpret Hosea's prophecy, for instance, do we mean Hosea's intended meaning or God's?

Now some scholars argue that there is no problem here. The human author's meaning is the same as God's. Well-known evangelical Old Testament scholar Walter Kaiser makes this point strongly and almost persuasively.[11] He rightly attempts to guard against an arbitrary form of exegesis that reads into biblical texts hidden or spiritual meanings that are not there and even conflict with the obvious meaning of the written word. However, the strict connection that Kaiser draws between human and divine intention in a biblical text makes it very difficult to explain some of the later biblical interpretations of earlier prophecy. A striking example is the use of Hosea 11:1 in Matthew 2:15.

In the latter part of the Book of Hosea the prophet is presenting a case against Israel. Writing in the eighth century B.C., he is serving as God's lawyer and accusing them of great crimes against the Lord. The punishment for these crimes would eventually take the form of Assyrian conquest of the northern kingdom in 722 B.C. As part of his case, Hosea recalls God's gracious rescue of Israel from Egyptian bondage: "When Israel was a child, I loved him as a son, and I called my son out of Egypt" (Hos. 11:1). There is no doubt what Hosea has in mind. His intention is clearly to invoke the exodus, a historical event which took place centuries before his time, in order to make the Israel of his own day even more culpable in their rebellion. This is no forward-looking prophecy.

However, when we turn to the Gospel of Matthew, we witness what strikes us at first as an amazing use of Hosea's words.

The context here is the birth and infancy of Jesus Christ. After
the wise men left, Joseph and Mary did not take Jesus back to
Nazareth, but slipped down to Egypt. They took this precaution
because God had revealed to them that they were in danger from
Herod. After Herod's death they returned to Palestine, and it is
at this point that Matthew notes, "This fulfilled what the Lord
had spoken through the prophet, 'I called my Son out of Egypt.'"

At first, we are taken aback. Nothing in Hosea prepares us for
Matthew's use of the old prophet's words. However, upon reflection it makes sense. As we read Matthew 2:15 in the light of the
Book of Matthew as a whole and the Bible in its entirety, we see
that God has drawn an analogy between Israel, God's son, being
freed from Egypt, and Jesus, God's Son, coming up out of Egypt.
This analogy, which is observed by careful readers of the Gospel,
reminds us to allow room in our hermeneutic theory and practice for what the Bible itself clearly demonstrates: God's intention may surpass the conscious intention of the human author.
The ultimate meaning of a passage resides in the intention of the
ultimate Author.

Distinguishing between divine and human intention does not
lead to the subjectivity and arbitrariness about which Kaiser worries. In the first place, the ultimate meaning of a passage is never
at odds with the human intention; rather, it is an extension thereof.
Second, we cannot appeal to the divine intention of a passage
apart from the prodding of the Bible itself. It is actually the canon
that set up the analogy between Jesus and the exodus. Indeed,
Matthew does not here suggest that Jesus' being brought out
from Egypt fulfilled a messianic prophecy found in one verse of
Hosea, but that this event fit into a whole pattern of fulfilment:
Jesus is himself the exodus.

We have identified four contemporary popular and academic
challenges to the primary hermeneutical task of discovering the
author's intended meaning in a passage or book of the Bible. (1)
We do not know the authors of a number of Old Testament

books. (2) Some Old Testament books were written over a period of time by ~~more than one author~~. (3) ~~We know nothing about any of the authors~~ of the Old Testament except through their writings. In any case, all the human authors of the Old Testament are dead and obviously cannot be questioned or interviewed to illuminate us about the intentions of their writings. And then, most importantly, (4) the Bible itself informs us that ~~God stands behind the human authors~~ and that sometimes the human authors wrote better than they knew.

In order to meet these challenges and refute the skepticism of critics like Clines, we must present a more sophisticated understanding of what we are doing in interpretation. What do we really mean when we say that our goal is the author's intended meaning? To answer this question, we need to visualize the dynamic process through which God's revelation is communicated:

~~God—human author—BIBLICAL TEXT—first readers→ present-day readers~~

Through the biblical text messages are sent from the author(s) to the reader(s). Ultimately, the Bible is a message from God to us. We read the Bible, therefore, to discover what God intends to tell us today.

Now God did not dictate his message to us in a mechanical fashion. Nor did he speak his word in a transcultural manner (whatever that might be), but in a way that was immediately understood by its first readers. God's revelation was specifically addressed to Israelites. It was written in Hebrew, and its human authors made use of their own style as well as native literary and cultural conventions. Theologically, we might think of the text as an incarnational model of revelation. Just as the Word of God came bodily to the world as a specific Palestinian Jewish male, so the Word of God written assumed a ~~culturally specific~~ form in the Bible.

Clearly, God's act of communication through the Bible is not
a simple, cut-and-dried affair, a fact that has practical implications.
The first is that we must study the text thoroughly. Though our
goal is the author's intention, we gain access to the author only
through his text. Since the Author/author(s) spoke in the language and idiom of the ancient Near East, we must become
~~acquainted with the Hebrew language and the broad literary and
cultural conventions of the day.~~ We must not read the Bible as
if it had been written yesterday. This means, in effect, that in our
reading we must first ~~travel back in time (through our imaginations) and approach the text as if we were the first readers~~.
~~But then we must read the Bible from our present situations.~~
When we do this, we will note that we come to the Bible not from
different, contradictory places, but from different, complemen-
tary places. As a white, middle-class American and professional
Reformed theologian, I will attend to some aspects of the text and
miss others. Another individual, say, a Latin American layperson
living under an oppressive state government, will note other things.
That is, ~~our different situations will attract us to different aspects
of God's message. So, then, we ought to read the Bible in community.~~ Sometimes our interpretations will contradict each other;
in that case one of us will probably be wrong, but we also need to
be open to the possibility that we both may be right.

As we examine the biblical text from our own personal situations, we must not give up our goal to discover the author's
intention, ultimately God's intention. Otherwise, the Bible
becomes meaningless as a religious document. It no longer is
God's Word to us. Our hermeneutical task, then, is obviously no
simple proposition.

Two last words on the subject. First, some might think that
our recommended approach will end up in confusion and uncertainty. Keep in mind, however, that what the Bible considers
important it does not say once or twice, but hundreds and even
thousands of times. We cannot miss the basic message of the

Bible, which is the way of salvation. Here ~~the doctrine of perspicuity comes into play. The Bible is absolutely clear on our spiritual problem and the solution to that problem, which of course is the gospel.~~

However, we must also admit that there are interpretive issues in the Bible that are not so clearly answered. To pick just two of many, let's consider the hotly debated issues of the "days" of Genesis and the role of the millennium. These topics are debated because ~~the Bible is not concerned to be clear about them. Such issues, while they should be studied and debated, must not be allowed to become a matter of fracture within the church~~.

Second, some may wonder why we have restricted the goal of interpretation to the meaning of the text. Why haven't we spoken of the text's significance to us as individuals or to society as a second important goal? The fact is that we have. It may be possible to distinguish meaning from application on a strictly theoretical level, but it is never possible to do so in practice. For one thing, such a separation would demand that we approach the text as an object out there to be dissected before it is appropriated into our lives. It would ask us to be scientists in the interpretive task and to study the Bible objectively. But such study of the Bible is neither possible nor desired. It is not possible because we cannot make ourselves blank slates. We cannot fully divest ourselves of our presuppositions and concerns, some of which are so embedded in us that we have no awareness of them. It is folly to think we can approach the biblical text without some preunderstanding. But perhaps even more cogent is the fact that it would be undesirable, even sinful, to try to read the Bible objectively. God desires us to come to his Word with our questions, our adoration, our struggles, our worship.

But what of the danger of reading our prejudices into the Bible? ~~The history of the church is filled with people who consciously or unconsciously perverted the message of the Bible to fit their own needs.~~ Many slave owners and slave traders, for

instance, were devout Christians who believed the Bible justi-
fied their activities. On the other hand, there are a number of
stories, most recently from Latin America, of oppressed Christians using the Bible to justify violent armed overthrow of the
rich classes.

Actually, we ought not divest ourselves of our prejudices when
we read the Bible. Rather, we should be as aware of them as we
can and submit them to the Word. We must allow the Bible to
critique us rather than put ourselves in the position of criticiz-
ing the Bible. We must be as objective as we can with regard to
our subjectivity and always aware that there is more under the
surface. We are back again to the important point of reading in
community. Further, we must fully embrace the idea that meaning includes significance. We cannot truly understand a biblical
passage with just our head, but must involve our heart and our
actions as well.

Principle 2: Read Scripture in Its Context

The Bible is a special book. It is the only book that comes
ultimately from God. It thus has an authority that far surpasses
that of any other book. However, we must not let its uniqueness
obscure the fact that the Bible in other ways is a book like any
other book. God chose to communicate his revelation to us in
literary forms that we recognize from other written works. And
keeping the Bible's literary nature in mind, we need to remember that the most basic of all principles in reading literature is
to read in context.

The principle of reading in context certainly makes sense, and
most of us will affirm the need to so read the Bible, at least on a
theoretical level, but many of us fail to do so in practice. Our failure has more to do with laziness than anything else. We give the
Word of God only a snippet of our time, so we end up reading
only a snippet, that is, a few verses here and there. Since we don't
know Scripture well enough to have a sense of the whole, we end

up extracting nuggets out of God's gold mine of truth. The problem is, extracting Scripture from its context often results in mis-
understanding and misapplication of the Word of God.

To read a passage of Scripture in context is simply to read it
with a sense of its place in the whole. This is, on the one hand,
one of the easiest of our hermeneutical principles and takes the
least amount of time. But on the other hand, it takes a lifetime.
This is true because the Bible is unfathomably rich. So rich that
no one can master the Scripture in a lifetime. There is always
something more to know, something more to learn from God's
Word. And it is precisely from our knowledge of the whole that
we must read the part.

Levels of Context

Some people misunderstand context to refer strictly to the
paragraphs immediately before a passage and the verses right
after it. That is where we start but we do not end there. Context may be envisioned as a series of concentric circles emanat-
ing from the passage presently being read. An apt comparison is
the ever-expanding circles of waves going out from the center
point when one throws a rock into a pond.

The most basic level of context is the near context, that is, the
words, sentences, and paragraphs that lead up to and follow the
text in question. While the nature of the near context will differ
from genre to genre, it will usually give the flow of thought and
emotion that leads up to and follows the passage being studied.

The next level of context is the section and book. Rarely do
we have time to sit down and read a whole book of the Old Testament (or at least we don't think we do). We must keep in mind,
however, that the human author is not communicating a series
of pithy thoughts to his audience, but a message that can be cap-
tured only on the level of his whole work. If we are studying Micah
4:1–5, for instance, we need to have a sense of the whole prophecy
of Micah to know where our passage fits in.

How can we do this, especially if we are novice readers of Scripture? Here is one of many situations in which reference works like introductions to the Old Testament or commentaries can aid us.[12] These works often provide an overview of the message of the prophet as well as an outline. Thus we can see where our passage fits into the whole book. With some of the longer books of the Old Testament, we may also want to talk about an intermediary level of context. That is, it may be advisable to investigate how our passage fits into a major section of the book before we proceed to the context of the book as a whole.

At a more general level there is the context of the Testament. There was such a radical transformation with the coming of Jesus Christ that we must first expend some energy coming to know how our passage fits in with the whole Old Testament. We are at this point beginning to understand that the Bible is an organic unity. The different books of the Bible may have been written by different people at different times, but the ultimate Author was telling one story to which the different parts all contribute.

Finally, there is the context of the canon. We must ultimately understand that any passage must be read in the light of the whole. The Old Testament is not a self-enclosed body of literature; rather, it ends with the expectation of a coming fulfilment. As Christians we believe that that fulfilment is Jesus Christ, and that the New Testament is the God-breathed account and interpretation of that fulfilment. Not surprisingly, then, we will see that the New Testament understands itself to be the articulation of the ultimate meaning of the Old.

Let's illustrate the different levels of context with a look at a passage of Scripture. Any passage will do, but we will choose Genesis 39:9: "No one here has more authority than I do! He has held back nothing from me except you, because you are his wife. How could I ever do such a wicked thing? It would be a great sin against God." It is obvious that we can't understand much about this verse without the near context, which begins with the paragraph and continues to the end of the chapter. Indeed, without the near context, we don't know who is speaking, to whom he is speaking, nor the nature of the "wicked thing" that is at issue. Reading the verse in its near context, we see that the speaker is Joseph, the son of Jacob who found himself in Egypt because of the treachery of his brothers; the person to whom he is speaking is Potiphar's wife; and the "wicked thing" is her proposal of a sexual tryst behind her husband's back.

There is far more to this story than we can write about here, but we will at least point out that Joseph is a paradigm for how someone in a close relationship with God should act when tempted. Joseph understands that to agree to sleep with this woman would be a betrayal not only of her husband, who trusted him, but, more importantly, of God, who, the passage emphasizes again and again, is the cause of his prosperity. Unfortunately for Joseph, at least in the short term, godly resistance lands him in jail. But even there God demonstrates clearly that he is still with Joseph: "The chief jailer had no more worries after that, because Joseph took care of everything. The LORD was with him, making everything run smoothly and successfully" (39:23).

Turning to the level of section and book, we find that Genesis 39 is one episode in the broader story of Joseph, which is found in chapters 37 through 50. Technically, Genesis 38 departs from the account of Joseph to tell the story of Judah, another of Jacob's sons, and Tamar. For this reason some people prefer to think of this section as the story of Jacob's sons, but that should not detract from recognizing that Joseph is the focus of attention in the vast majority of this part of the Book of Genesis.

In the context of the Joseph story, Joseph has in Genesis 39 just arrived in Egypt, having been violently rejected by his brothers and sold into slavery. As we read the chapters that follow, we quickly note a pattern. Joseph seems blown about by the winds of fortune, but wherever he is, God makes him successful. And these events move him closer and closer to the center of Egyptian power.

From jail he moves into the service of Pharaoh, which results in his elevation to second in importance in the kingdom. From this position he is eventually reconciled to his family and provides them with the means to survive a severe famine in the area.

In the last chapter of the story we find a speech that helps us understand the overall purpose of the various threads of Joseph's life, including his being framed by Potiphar's wife. After the death of their father Jacob, Joseph's brothers are afraid. After all, they had made his life miserable by their jealousy, anger, and hate. Now that their father is dead, the time for Joseph's vengeance has come. Accordingly, the brothers cringe before Joseph to beg his forgiveness and mercy. This allows him the opportunity to share his perception of the purpose of his life: "Don't be afraid of me. Am I God, to judge and punish you? As far as I am concerned, God turned into good what you meant for evil. He brought me to the high position I have today so I could save the lives of many people" (Gen. 50:19–20).

In light of Joseph's speech we must go back to Genesis 39. Yes, this chapter provides a paradigm of how to act when facing temptation. But there is more here. Genesis 39 is a concrete illustration of God's overruling the evil of other people, using it instead to bring about a great rescue, a salvation.

Now we need to go from the immediate section (chs. 37–50) to the Book of Genesis as a whole. We will highlight the most important point. Genesis is divided into three clear sections: (1) the primeval history (chs. 1–11); (2) the patriarchal narrative (chs. 12–36); and (3) the story of Joseph (chs. 37–50). In Genesis 1–11 the camera's focus is on the world, and the story ends with catastrophe and human failure to respond to God's continuing mercy. Genesis 12 then opens a whole new episode as the camera's focus narrows to one man through whom God will bring salvation to the world. This is Abraham, the father of the faith, to whom God delivers a command followed by a promise: "Leave your country, your relatives, and your father's house, and go to the land that I will show you. I will cause you to become the father of a great nation. I will bless you and make you famous, and I will make you a blessing to others. I will bless those who bless you and curse those who curse you. All the families of the earth will be blessed through you" (Gen. 12:1–3). This command and promise reverberate through the rest of the Book of Genesis and beyond, and we can already see the relevance for Genesis 39 and the Joseph story. The imprisonment of Joseph is a key part of his elevation to a position of power eventually enabling him to rescue his family. But, and this is the crucial point, this is no ordinary family; this is the family of promise, the one through whom salvation and blessing will come to the rest of the world.

Because of the rescue of Joseph's family, the story of God's promises can continue in the context of the Testament. A nation is born out of this family after making the sojourn into Egypt. God then shows his power and grace by bringing them into the Promised Land. The Old Testament is an account of the threats to and fulfilments of the promises of Genesis 12:1–3. Closely related is the ultimate textual context, the canon as a whole. Into the family and nation of promise, who were so dramatically spared by Joseph, is born Jesus Christ, who brings salvation to the world. For the Christian this is the most necessary and theologically rich level.

Types of Context

It is always essential to read a biblical passage in its context. It is equally essential to realize that context is a flexible concept as we move from book to book of the Bible. We examined in some detail the context of Genesis 39, an example of historical prose, a narrative set in the context of ever-larger stories. Moving very easily from the immediate context to the broad context, we saw how this single event fits into the larger complex.

But with passages like Proverbs 10:1, we cannot understand context in precisely the same way. Proverbs does not tell a story;

it presents wisdom principles. A close examination of the structure of the Book of Proverbs will show that 10:1 stands at a moment of transition, a transition from extended wisdom discourses that may be as long as a whole chapter to the presentation of a series of pithy proverbs that usually occupy a single verse, but may occasionally extend to a handful of verses.

As we read Proverbs 10–31 we note that, although proverbs on the same general topic may occasionally appear together, more often than not the proverbs proceed from one topic to another without any apparent connection between them. In the verses immediately following 10:1, for example, which speaks of wise and foolish children, we encounter proverbs on "ill-gotten gain" (v. 2), on hunger (v. 3), and on laziness (vv. 4, 5). Accordingly, whenever I preach on a proverb, I do not choose five verses that follow one on another. Rather, I will select scattered proverbs that concern a particular topic. I will certainly look at the immediate context to see if anything there will help me understand the proverb of my particular interest, but the immediate context is usually less illuminating than the other proverbs on the same subject. On the other hand, we must not understand individual proverbs in isolation, even though they give the impression of being motto-like. It is crucial to understand the dynamic of the entire Book of Proverbs to get the theological message of the individual proverb, and that dynamic is largely determined from context.

In a nutshell, the discourses of Proverbs 1–9 create a context in which to understand the pithy proverbs of 10–31. The discourses present a series of metaphors which climax in chapters 8 and 9. The basic metaphor is the image of life as a path. The reader, who in the book's ancient context is male, is walking the path of life. He encounters various helps and hindrances along the way. His father-teacher warns him, for instance, of the possibility of ambush (Prov. 1:11, 18). He is told that he will encounter temptations that will lure him off the path. The prime temptation is the strange woman, the adulteress, who will try to seduce him to his great harm (Prov. 5 and 7). But there is another woman, Wisdom herself, who urges the reader to follow her on the path.

The two women are most fully described in the climactic chapters. Wisdom (8:1–9:6) is a woman characterized by righteousness, truth, justice, prudence, and many other virtues. On the other hand, Folly (9:13–18) is a woman who is brash, ignorant, and deceptive. Each woman calls out to the reader, the man on the path, to come join her for dinner and a serious relationship (cf. 9:4–6 and 9:16–17).

Who are these women? They both live on a hill (9:3, 14). This is the clue we need to solve the riddle of their identity. In the ancient Near East the only building on the high point of a city was its temple. Thus Lady Wisdom is a metaphor for the true God himself; Folly, on the contrary, represents all the spurious gods and goddesses that tempted the Israelites into false religion.

That Proverbs 10:1 is a deeply religious verse can be seen only in context. Wise children bring joy to their parents. That means they have joined themselves with Lady Wisdom; they follow the true God—they worship Yahweh. But foolish children bring grief to their parents by worshiping idols. The implications are unmistakable: those who embrace Wisdom find knowledge and life (9:6), while those who follow Folly will end up in the grave (9:18).

From our brief look at Proverbs 10:1, we readily see that we must be sensitive to the different types of literary context in the Old Testament. For this verse necessitates an approach totally unlike our examination of Genesis 39. In other words, we must attend to the genre of the book we are studying.

Principle 3: Identify the Genre of the Book and Passage

On the one hand, the Bible, as its name implies, is a single book. But on the other, the Bible is an anthology, a veritable library of books. And just like a library there are many different kinds of books. Libraries and bookstores usually arrange their books according to literary type. One shelf may have biographies, another novels, yet a third travel books. Each different kind of book, each literary type, constitutes a separate genre.

"Genre," a term derived from French, is related to our English words "general" and "generalization." A genre of literature is a group of texts associated with one another by virtue of similarities. In other words, a genre is an abstraction, a generalization if you will, regarding specific concrete texts. The similarities that bind these texts together may be of many different types. The texts may be alike in their content, their structure, their mood, their phraseology, or some combination thereof.

The Bible includes a variety of ancient genres. On one level we can divide the Bible into two genres: prose narrative and poetry. But on an even more constructive level we can speak of ~~history, law, lyric poetry, wisdom literature, prophecy, and apocalyptic~~ That each of these categories can be further divided into subgenres highlights an important characteristic of genre: it is a flexible concept.[13] Genres do not fall out of heaven. They are habits of writing and reading that can be stretched out or changed over time.

~~The Genre of Individual Books~~

Before we discuss genre identification in the study of biblical texts, we must first understand a bit more from the perspective of the dynamic process through which God communicates his revelation to us (God—human author—BIBLICAL TEXT—first readers—present-day readers). The text takes shape from the action of its author and intends to impact the behavior of the reader. But to make his work understood, the author must write in a conventional way, that is, in a way that has precursors. Authors don't sit down to write just anything at all; they sit down to write a novel or a biography. Their writing takes a certain form because they know what a novel looks like, what a biography contains. Their writing thus contains signals that communicate to the readers what it is that they are getting. And in this process the genre evokes a reading strategy. It subtly informs readers how to take the words in front of them.

An example will be useful. One evening I began to read a story and was jarred by its opening sentence: "As Gregor Samsa awoke from an uneasy sleep, he found himself transformed into a gigantic insect." A striking sentence, but it didn't completely shake me, for the story, "Metamorphosis," was published in a collection of the surreal fiction of Franz Kafka. My recognition of the genre told me how to take Kafka's writing.

Now while it's true that we have nothing quite like Kafka in the Old Testament, our identification of the genre of a particular biblical book or passage will radically affect how we understand and apply it. The history of the interpretation of the Song of Songs provides an excellent example.

After a one-verse superscription the Song begins: "Kiss me again and again, for your love is sweeter than wine. How fragrant your cologne, and how pleasing your name! No wonder all the young women love you! Take me with you. Come, let's run! Bring me into your bedroom, O my king" (1:2–4a). These are passionate words from an unnamed woman to a man. They are the stuff of love poetry, and indeed that is how virtually every scholar today approaches the Song of Songs as a whole. Although there are many differences in interpretation,[14] there is vast agreement that the Song is love poetry. This consensus is, however, a relatively recent phenomenon.

Early rabbinic and Christian interpretation viewed the Song of Songs as a different genre. It was not love poetry. After all, why would a book dedicated to the lusts of the flesh be in the Holy Scriptures? No, the Song must be something other than it appears to be on the surface; it must be some sort of allegory.

Now, not all allegorical interpretation is wrong-minded, and indeed we know, from the interpretation of Jesus himself, that at least some of the parables of the New Testament are allegories.

The problem with treating the Song of Songs as an allegory is that the book itself contains not a single hint that it is an allegory. Thus allegorical interpretations of the Song yield arbitrary results. Reading it as a historical allegory, for instance, identifies Song of Songs 1:2–4a with the exodus from Egypt. The king is none other than God, and the woman is his bride Israel. God is going to take his bride Israel away from Egypt and bring her into his bedroom (the Promised Land), where he will have an intimate relationship with her.

Early Christian interpretation was equally arbitrary in its assignment of meaning to the events and characters of the book. The Song of Songs was reinterpreted as a hymn celebrating the relationship between Jesus and his bride the church, and the details of the book were understood accordingly. When early interpreter Cyril of Alexandria read Song of Songs 1:13, "My lover is like a sachet of myrrh lying between my breasts," he thought the two breasts represented the Old and New Testaments. The sachet was Christ, who spanned both!

The Song is an excellent example of how genre (mis)identification affects interpretive strategy and also application. The old way of reading the Song as an allegory prohibited studying the book to gain insight into contemporary male-female relationships. Though intended to help husbands and wives relate to one another,[15] the Song was used purely for theological purposes.

Of course, genre (mis)identification does not arise out of thin air. The allegorical reading was driven by the importation of a Platonic body-soul dualism into Jewish and Christian theology. The Bible appealed to the soul; sex was a matter of the body—thus the Song of Songs could not be about sex. Allegory was a genre that allowed readers to take the Song as meaning something other than what appeared on the surface. As time wore on, however, this arbitrary and unsubstantiated reading of the book became harder and harder to maintain. In the nineteenth century came the discovery of similar texts from Egypt and Mesopotamia that provided strong empirical evidence that the Song was love poetry.

But even this is not the end of the story. Interpretive debate continues that at bottom is a debate about genre. Is the Song a drama? Does it have a plot? And if so, are there two main characters or three? Is it a collection of love poetry, an erotic psalter, if you will? Satisfactory answers will come only from a close reading of the text itself.

We need to raise here a note of caution. Much mischief can go on under the rubric of genre. To take one notable example, it is insufficient, in attempts to solve apparent contradictions with modern science, to simply assert that Genesis 1 is myth or parable. To prove this contention, one needs to point to indicators of the genre within the text itself. But close study reveals that the chapter is prophetic narrative like the rest of the Book of Genesis. Indeed, we move from Genesis 1 through the rest of the book with no radical shift in generic tone.

On the other hand, we cannot always be dogmatic in our genre analysis. In other words, the generic signals are not always unambiguous. Job is a good example. Job is clearly a wisdom text, taking the form of a debate about the source of all wisdom. It is unclear, however, whether the book intends to be historical. It tells a story, but does the author expect his audience to consider the events as actually having taken place in space and time?

Now the first few lines of a text are often critical for genre identification, since they set the tone for what follows. And the opening of the Book of Job offers strong evidence of historicity. The first verse of Job is similar to the opening verses of Judges 17 and 1 Samuel 1, two passages with an indubitable intention to communicate historical events. We might also take as supporting evidence what appears to be a witness to the historicity of the person Job in the biblical Book of Ezekiel. In 14:14, 20, the prophet mentions Job along with two other historical figures from the Old Testament, Noah and Daniel.

Although outside of the book that bears his name there is no way to prove or disprove Job's existence—for instance, through archeological attestation—we can conclude that there is a definite historical intention. We are to understand Job to be a real person who lived in the past and who suffered. Nonetheless, the question of the historical precision of the book remains. That is, although Job intends to be historical, other genre signals from the book indicate that precision is not a high priority. For instance, the dialogues are all cast in poetic form. Since people do not normally speak to one another in poetic form (especially when in extreme distress), we clearly have nothing like transcripts of the conversations that took place between the characters of the book. Thus they may be accurate without being precise. The purpose in using poetry for these speeches was to elevate the book from a specific historical event to a story with universal application. The Book of Job is not simply a historical chronicle; it is wisdom that is to be applied to all who read it.

The Genre of Individual Passages

It is vital, in the first place, to identify the genre of the book as a whole. But it is also vital to identify the form of individual passages within a book as accurately as possible. Let's take as our example a single verse, Nahum 3:1, which translates literally:

> Woe, murderous city,
> totally deceptive,
> full of plunder;
> prey does not cease.

The genre of the Book of Nahum as a whole is divine war oracle.[16] The object of the prophet's invective is the Assyrian city of Nineveh. Nahum 3:1 forms an important part of his message of doom against that evil city.[17] The genre of this verse is identified by its first word, "woe" (Hebrew *hôy*). Contemporary scholars have given this common prophetic form (see, e.g., Isa. 5:18–19; Amos 5:18–20; 6:1–7; Mic. 2:1–5) the not surprising name "woe oracle."

Research into this genre, a subgenre of prophetic judgment oracles, has located its roots in a form of speech commonly heard in funeral processions (1 Kings 13:30; Jer. 22:18; 34:5; Amos 5:16).[18] As mourners followed a dead body on its way to the grave site, they would express their grief by crying, "*Hôy, hôy.*" The association of this word with death probably led the prophets to use it to presage destruction. In many of the prophetic uses, and certainly in the use here in Nahum, *hôy* no longer marks an expression of lamentation for the dead. On the contrary, Nahum is far from lamenting the coming destruction of vicious Nineveh. Indeed, he can hardly restrain his joy at the prospect. *Hôy* has become a threat or a curse directed against the enemies of God. This point indicates that genre identification is not so mechanical a procedure as many form-critical analyses would suggest; rather, the interpreter must be open to nuanced uses within different contexts.

Genre identification is an extremely useful, even vital, tool of interpretation—if used flexibly. Contrary to perceptions among biblical scholars of the late nineteenth and early twentieth centuries, genre is a fluid and flexible category.[19] It has more to do with the human propensity to group similar items than with any divinely instituted categorization.

One implication of genre fluidity is that the same text may reflect multiple genres. Remember that genre is a form of generalization or abstraction. As we identify a variety of texts with a specific genre, we focus on the similarities they share with each other. A genre can be broad, based on only a few traits in common, or narrow. In the latter case, which gets closer to the details of the text, there are many traits in common. This can be illustrated with a look at Psalm 98:

Sing a new song to the LORD,
　　for he has done wonderful deeds.
He has won a mighty victory
　　by his power and holiness.
The LORD has announced his victory
　　and has revealed his righteousness to every nation!
He has remembered his promise to love and be faithful to Israel.
　　The whole earth has seen the salvation of our God.

Shout to the LORD, all the earth;
　　break out in praise and sing for joy!
Sing your praise to the LORD with the harp,
　　with the harp and melodious song,
　　with trumpets and the sound of the ram's horn.
Make a joyful symphony before the LORD, the King!

Let the sea and everything in it shout his praise!
　　Let the earth and all living things join in.
　　Let the rivers clap their hands in glee!
　　Let the hills sing out their songs of joy before the LORD.
For the LORD is coming to judge the earth.
　　He will judge the world with justice,
　　and the nations with fairness.

We can describe the genre of Psalm 98 on many levels, starting with one of the broadest: poetry. The terseness of the lines,
parallelism between the versets, and high level of imagery signal
to us that the psalm is a poem. Psalm 98 is one of a large number of poems in the Hebrew Bible, not only in the Psalms, but
also the prophets, other wisdom books, even the Pentateuch and
historical books (e.g., the victory songs of Exod. 15 and Judg. 5).
At another level we see that Psalm 98, like all the psalms, is lyric
poetry connected with the worship institutions of ancient Israel
as opposed to the dramatic poetry of Job and the narrative poetry
of Exodus 15.

Perhaps the most illuminating generic analysis of Psalm 98 takes place on the more narrow levels. Here we can do little more than name them. Psalm 98 is a hymn celebrating a robust relationship with God, as opposed to the also common laments and thanksgivings. Of the many types of hymns, Psalm 98 is one which specifically praises God as a warrior who has saved his people in the past, rules over them in the present, and is coming to judge their enemies in the future. As a hymn of victory celebrating the divine warrior, it is to be sung after the battle, not before it (as, e.g., Ps. 7) or during it (Ps. 91). At its narrowest level, Psalm 98 is most like Psalm 96.[20]

Principle 4: Consider the Historical and Cultural Background of the Bible

The Bible is not a transcultural document. If it were, then no human being could relate to it or even understand it. Rather, God spoke his Word to us in a language we can clearly understand. In a phrase, the Bible is God's Word incarnate. It is divine speech which has taken on human form. And just as we must focus on both the divinity and humanity of the incarnate Second Person of the Trinity, we must be careful not to neglect either aspect of the Bible. That is, we must never treat it as a purely human document as if it were like every other book. Nor must we treat it as a purely divine book, as if it had fallen out of heaven. As Jesus is like us except without sin, so the Bible is like a human literary work, but without error.

When we pick up the Bible and read it with eyes of faith, we cannot fail to marvel at both aspects. But we are particularly interested here in exploring the human aspect. While mindful that we cannot completely separate the divine and the human, we see immediately that God chose to communicate his Word to us in an incarnational manner. The Bible is not in the language of angels; it is in Hebrew. Now Hebrew is a wonderful language, but it is no closer to God than is English, French,

Russian, or Korean. It is not the language we will speak in heaven, contrary to the thoughts of some earlier theologians. But because God used the language that his people spoke at the time of his revelation, we, living centuries later, must learn that ancient language and then translate it into our modern tongues before we can even get a start on hearing God speak to us. Most modern readers forget this because Bible translations are so readily available.

But the need to acquaint ourselves with the historical and cultural background extends well beyond the level of language. God wrote his work in the genres of the day, using native literary conventions. He spoke to people who knew the priesthood and the monarchy, institutions which we do not have in our society. These facts remind us of the need to study the historical and cultural background of any book or passage that we are reading. Whenever we seek to understand the Bible according to its author's intention, we are to transport ourselves back into ancient times, the days of the first audience. We may indeed be able to understand the gist of a passage, but our comprehension becomes ever so much richer once we know the ancient backgrounds.

Principle 5: Consider the Grammar and Structure within the Passage

In addition to considering historical and cultural background, we must read our passage closely in all its detail. Look for items like connectors, verb tenses, and modifiers to nouns. Connectors (words like "but," "and," "therefore"), for instance, help give the reader the logical connection between words. Remember, though, that the meaning of the Bible is not in isolated words but in the context, namely, in sentences and paragraphs.

As an example, let's look at some of the grammatical and structural details that help us understand the words and clauses in Psalm 131. This poem has a special kind of structural feature, parallelism, that is, the clauses echo each other. The first clause makes a statement, which is then expanded upon in the following clauses. When reading a psalm, it will be helpful to reflect on how the parallelism contributes to its meaning.

The parallel structure (both in the meaning of the words and in the grammar) links the three clauses of verse 1 together:

> My heart is not proud, O LORD,
>   my eyes are not haughty;
> I do not concern myself with great matters
>   or things too wonderful for me. [NIV]

Careful attention to the structural relationship between the three clauses shows that David distances himself from pride in three distinct areas: his core personality (heart), his external demeanor (eyes), and his actions.

The "but" that begins the second verse draws a strong contrast between the pride described in the first verse and the attitude expressed in the second:

> But I have stilled and quieted my soul;
>   like a weaned child with its mother,
>   like a weaned child is my soul within me. [NIV]

The English translation of the Hebrew verbs ("have stilled" and "have quieted") indicates that David's confidence is rooted in the past and continues in the present. He then illustrates his present disposition by using the word "like." Note that David does not use a generic term for child, but the word for a weaned child. When we reflect on this choice, we realize that a weaned child, one that does not need its mother's milk, is especially calm in its mother's lap. It does not grasp for the source of sustenance, but rests quietly in its mother's arms.

The final verse of the psalm uses an imperative to drive home the application of the truths presented in the first two verses:

O Israel, put your hope in the LORD
both now and forevermore. [NIV]

Most Bible readers do not have access to the Hebrew text of the Old Testament or the Greek of the New Testament. Serious grammatical and syntactical study must be based on the original languages, however. For that reason, it is helpful to have a copy of a very literal translation like the New American Standard Bible for serious study. Indeed, the best way to get a feel for the original text is to compare a number of different translations. A good commentary based on the Hebrew and Greek text is also invaluable for insight into the grammatical and structural relationships.

Principle 6: Interpret Experience in the Light of Scripture, not Scripture in the Light of Experience

Each of us comes to the Bible with a rich background. Our upbringing, education, and various life experiences all shape who we are. We earlier observed (p. 31) that it is neither possible nor desirable to divest ourselves of our experience when we read the Bible. But at the same time it is crucial for us to let Scripture shape our experience rather than allow our experience to shape our understanding of Scripture. The Bible is God's Word to us, and we need to hear what God has to say about our life. If we simply read the Bible in a self-justifying way, we will not allow the power of God to transform us.

I recently had dinner with a pastor who illustrated the dangers of interpreting Scripture in light of personal experience. Our discussion centered on the question whether spiritual gifts like prophecy, supernatural healing, and tongues have continued beyond the New Testament period to today. Now I am not interested here in tackling this difficult question, but merely in questioning my friend's approach to the issue. He had been criticized by a fellow minister whose denomination does not believe in the continuance of the spiritual gifts in the church today. To this my friend responded with passion: "I can't deny what happened to me five years ago. I was really sick, and I was really depressed. I prayed to God, and all of a sudden I found myself speaking in an unknown angelic language for thirty minutes. I was healed of my sickness. After that experience I cannot believe the Bible teaches the cessation of tongues." Regardless of the ultimate truth or error of his conclusion, my friend's reasoning was all wrong. It did not take into account the fact that we have deeply deceptive hearts (Jer. 17:9) that fool us into imposing our own feelings and desires onto the Bible. I am not suggesting that his experience should not make him more open to the continuance of tongues and miraculous healing, but that his next step should have been a new look at the biblical texts that bear on the question. Unfortunately, that is not what happened.

There is just as much fault at the other end of the spectrum. Early in my own Christian walk I became a staunch opponent of the belief that people can be possessed by demonic forces. My reasons? I had seen so many abuses, for instance, a friend of mine who did not need an exorcism so much as a good drug-rehabilitation program. Such experiences should lead us to renewed investigation of the Bible, but should never dictate our final conclusion. Misuse of the Bible is the result. Think of the South African advocates of apartheid who ripped the Bible out of context to support destructive and oppressive racial segregation. In addition, capitalists and Marxists alike marshal isolated biblical texts to support their own preconceptions. The proper procedure is to read the Bible self-critically and in community. Unfortunately, this is not an easy principle to exercise because there are difficult questions in the Bible that allow for some leeway in interpretation.

Principle 7: Always Seek the Full Counsel of Scripture

We should never read Scripture in isolation from the whole. For while many human authors contributed to the Bible, God is the ultimate Author of the whole. While the Bible is an anthology of many books, it is also one book. While it has many stories to tell, they all contribute to a single story.

The principle of seeking the full counsel of Scripture has important implications. First, we should never base doctrine or moral teachings on an obscure passage. The most important ideas in the Bible are stated hundreds of times. So we must not attach too much significance to a text that teaches something that is obscure or difficult and unsupported by other passages.

Second, if one passage seems to teach something, but another passage clearly teaches something else, we must understand the former in terms of the latter. That is, we must determine the meaning of the unclear verse by examining the clear teaching of Scripture.

A number of years ago I was asked to debate a popular radio teacher on the subject of Christ's return. He had just published a lengthy book arguing that Jesus was going to come again in 1994. The debate never would have occurred if he and his supporters had simply sought the full counsel of Scripture. While they had all kinds of convoluted mathematical arguments based on obscure interpretations of Scripture, they ignored the clear teaching of Mark 13:32: "However, no one knows the day or hour when these things will happen, not even the angels in heaven or the Son himself. Only the Father knows." Just reading that verse should have stopped all the manipulating of biblical passages to try to find out what is not for us to know.

Principle 8: Discover How the Scripture Passage Presents Jesus Christ

In order to grasp the full counsel of Scripture (principle 7), which is really the logical extension of reading a Bible passage in its context (principle 2), we need to study the themes and analogies that stretch from Genesis to Revelation. Then, when we read any one passage, we will be able to understand its place in the unfolding history of salvation.

This principle is particularly important as we read the Old Testament. After all, when walking on the road to Emmaus with two unnamed disciples, Jesus himself indicated that the whole Old Testament, not just a handful of messianic prophecies, looks forward to his coming: "He said to them, 'How foolish you are, and how slow of heart to believe all that the prophets have spoken! Did not the Christ have to suffer these things and then enter his glory?' And beginning with Moses and all the Prophets, he explained to them what was said in all the Scriptures concerning himself" (Luke 24:25–27 NIV). And later he remarked to other disciples: "This is what I told you while I was still with you: Everything must be fulfilled that is written about me in the Law of Moses, the Prophets and the Psalms" (Luke 24:44 NIV).

Take as an example of a passage that is anticipated in the Old Testament Matthew 4:1–11, which describes Jesus' temptation in the wilderness. If we keep the whole of Scripture in view as we read, Jesus' spending forty days and forty nights in the wilderness may remind us of the Israelites' forty-year trek in the wilderness. But the comparison goes beyond the number forty. The Israelites were tempted in the same three areas in which Jesus was tempted: (1) hunger and thirst; (2) testing God; and (3) worshiping false gods. Jesus, however, showed himself to be the obedient Son of God where the Israelites were disobedient. Indeed, Jesus responded to the temptations by quoting Deuteronomy (8:3; 6:16, 13), the sermon that Moses delivered to the Israelites at the end of their forty-year sojourn (see Matt. 4:4, 7, 10). So, then, reading Scripture in the light of the whole counsel of God not only prevents erroneous interpretations, but also gives us deeper insight into the Word of God.

Principle 9: Be Open-minded and Tolerant of Other Interpretations

"God is a God of truth; error must not be tolerated. Our Bible is inerrant. To adopt a mistaken view about the Bible is the worst error one can make." These and similar statements have been the foundation of much intolerance not only toward those outside of the church but, perhaps especially, toward those in the church. Those who are intolerant would do well to remember that while in its main teachings (e.g., our sinful nature and need of a Savior) the Bible is very clear, ~~it is not intended to answer with certainty all of our questions about God, life, ourselves, and others~~. We are left with some fuzzy edges, and what the Bible leaves unclear we must respect with open-mindedness and tolerance.

How long did creation take? When was the world created? Is the Book of Jonah a historical account or a parable? Under what conditions is divorce permissible? What do the thousand years in Revelation 20 signify? Is tongues a contemporary manifestation of the Spirit? Can women be ordained? These are important issues that need to be studied hard and discussed in community so that positions can be adopted. But while we are doing all this, we must acknowledge that God in his wisdom has not made the answers clear in his Word. Accordingly, we must ~~embrace those with whom we disagree~~ and carry on our discussions with them in the rich love of Christian fellowship. While we are called to make decisions, we must be sure to exercise ~~exegetical humility and tolerance~~ for other Christian viewpoints.

We have seen that we must be very careful in our interpretation and application of the unfathomably rich biblical text. The principles discussed in this chapter will serve well as basic guidelines for sound interpretation. Though not magical formulas, they will prevent us from the folly of trying to please ourselves by pouring our own desires and prejudices into our reading of the text.

Is the God of the Old Testament also the God of the New Testament?

Jesus turned to his disciples and said, "If someone slaps you on one cheek, turn the other cheek" (Luke 6:29). After the crossing of the Red Sea, Moses led the Israelites in a song that celebrated the great work God had just accomplished:

The LORD is a warrior;
    yes, the LORD is his name!
Pharaoh's chariots and armies
    he has thrown into the sea.
The very best of Pharaoh's officers
    have been drowned in the Red Sea.
The deep waters have covered them;
    they sank to the bottom like a stone. [Exod. 15:3–5]

At the end of his life as he was being horribly tortured on the cross, Jesus prays to his Father, "Forgive these people, because they don't know what they are doing" (Luke 23:34).

Back in the Old Testament, we hear the prophet Jeremiah speaking on behalf of God. Because his people have offended him, God addresses them not with words of forgiveness, but words of judgment: "I will make Jerusalem into a heap of ruins. . . . It will be a place haunted by jackals. The towns of Judah will be ghost towns, with no one living in them" (Jer. 9:11). Jeremiah does not speak alone. Most of the prophets proclaim equally harsh words of divine judgment.

Not surprisingly, many people feel that there is an insuperable gap between the Old and New Testament views of God. They emphasize the diversity between the Testaments and even claim that they contradict each other. The judgment, exclusion, and harshness of the Old Testament are contrasted with the salvation, inclusion, and compassion of the New. More pointedly, the warrior God who punishes in the Old Testament is contrasted with Jesus the suffering Messiah.

A movie that I saw in the early 1970s vividly illustrates this common (mis)conception. At the beginning of *The Ruling Class* Jack, a character played by Peter O'Toole, thinks he is Jesus and treats everyone with great kindness and benign generosity. The theme of the movie is that someone like Jesus cannot survive in contemporary society, and so Jack is consigned to a mental institution. For our purposes the most intriguing scene comes in the middle of the movie when a patient who thinks he is Yahweh, the God of the Old Testament, is brought into contact with Jack. This patient is the opposite of O'Toole's character. He is abrupt, rude, and violent, the stereotype that most people today, even Christians, associate with the God of the Old Testament.

Does the Bible describe God with this dichotomy? How can we relate the God of the Old Testament with the God of the New?

That is the subject of our second crucial question concerning the
Old Testament.

False Stereotypes

We must beware of falsely stereotyping both the God of the Old
Testament and the Jesus who is presented in the New. The God
of the Old Testament is not an arbitrary and purely dark figure,
and Jesus is not all flowers and light and soft goodness. Yahweh
never capriciously nor arbitrarily punished anyone. On the contrary, the witness of the Old Testament is consistent that he is a
"merciful and gracious God . . . slow to anger and rich in unfail-
ing love and faithfulness" (Exod. 34:6). He punished only after
repeated rebellion and insistent warnings. And he always had a
heart for the salvation of his people even when they grossly
offended him.

Perhaps the most powerful passage in this regard is presented
by the prophet Hosea. In view of Israel's repeated sins, God determines that the time has come to follow through on his repeated
threats to punish them. But as he does so, his heart is rent: "Oh,
how can I give you up, Israel? How can I let you go? How can I
destroy you like Admah and Zeboiim? My heart is torn within
me, and my compassion overflows. No, I will not punish you as
much as my burning anger tells me to. I will not completely
destroy Israel, for I am God and not a mere mortal. I am the Holy
One living among you, and I will not come to destroy" (Hos.
11:8–9). In light of this speech it is hard to maintain that the God
of the Old Testament is a heartless despot. The decision to punish his people tore him apart emotionally. We have a difficult time
comprehending this passage in part because we often forget that
our God is a God of intense passions.[1] Of course, he cannot be
swept away by the power of his emotions, but he is an emotional
being. Though Israel deserves eradication, his compassion simply will not allow him to follow through. Indeed, this intense love

for his human creatures provides the bridge to the greatest sacrifice of all time: the death of Christ on the cross.

As the God of the Old Testament is not a monolithic bully, so Jesus Christ is not totally passive or pacifist. In fact, his cleansing of the temple connects him to the Old Testament picture of divine judgment. When Jesus saw that God's house had been devoted to illegitimate commerce, he was totally outraged. Taking a whip, he forcibly drove the malefactors out. The scene inspired the Gospel writer to quote the psalmist's declaration, "Passion for God's house burns within me" (John 2:17, quoting Ps. 69:9).

Thus it is erroneous to make a distinct contrast between the Old and New Testament views of God. In the rest of this chapter we will explore the extremely varied presentation of God in the Old Testament, but in every instance see evidence of continuity as we move into the New. The God of the Old Testament is the God of the New.

Yahweh: The Center of the Bible

Of course, when we read the Bible, our first impression is one of diversity. We already observed in chapter 1 that the Bible was composed over a long period of time by many different human authors using various genres of writing. Sometimes it is hard to see the single story for all the stories being told. Yet there is an organic unity in the Bible. The clearest evidence is that we can speak of an ultimate Author. All of the Bible was originally inspired by God.

But there is also the question of the unity of the message of the Bible. Do its multiple voices sing in harmony, or is the Bible a cacophony of individual songs? Sometimes biblical scholars ask whether there is a center of biblical theology. Is there a single theme or motif under which all biblical revelation can be outlined? Some scholars have seen the center of biblical revelation in the covenant or the promises of God.[2] Others have seen it in the history of redemption or in God's design.[3] Many others, and their numbers have increased in recent years, would answer the question negatively. There is no center.

My own view falls somewhere in the middle. On the one hand, I do not believe that the Bible can be totally subsumed under any single theme. Those who offer the theme of the covenant as the center, for instance, struggle to situate the wisdom literature under that rubric.[4] However, there is a unifying theme, and that is God himself. To the question "What is the Bible about?" the obvious answer is that the Bible is about God.

However, if we stop with the simple observation that God is the center of the Bible, we really haven't said much. Among additional observations that we can make is that God never appears in the abstract. The Bible does not contain philosophical essays on the nature of God. We do not find the language of systematic theology or credal formulations. It is not that these are wrong or unhelpful, but that we do not find them in the Bible. We do not encounter words like hypostasis, Trinity, aseity, and apatheia. Rather, God is presented in the concreteness of vivid similes and metaphors. We read that God is a king, a teacher, a warrior, a shepherd, a parent, a spouse.

While the Bible never tells us why it presents God metaphorically, we can speculate. Vivid and concrete, metaphors arise out of everyday experience. Educated and illiterate, young and old, can grasp them. The Bible is not an elitist document; it is a book for all people. Even further, the metaphorical language of the Bible does more than inform our intellect. Imagery arouses our emotions in ways that plain prose cannot. Reading, for instance, that God is our father evokes a response that far surpasses what a prose equivalent could do.

In addition to being concrete, most of the leading metaphors of the Bible are relational. Of course, not all of them are. For instance,

God is a rock, a fortress (Ps. 18:1–2), a shield (Ps. 3:3), a light (Ps. 104:2), and a bird (Ps. 91:4). But most of the picture images of God entail a relationship. For instance, that God is pictured as the father (Ps. 68:5) and the mother (Ps. 131) of the faithful assumes that they are God's children. The image of God as Israel's husband (Hos. 1–3) implies that Israel is the wife. The Bible's acclamation that God is king understands his creatures to be his subjects. Through such metaphors of relationship the Bible reaches out to its readers in language that is not coldly abstract but warmly personal.

The Metaphor of Covenant King

We have been laying the groundwork to address the issue that concerns us: Is the God of the New Testament the same as the God of the Old? We will explore three relational metaphors that bind the Old and New Testaments together: God as covenant king; God as warrior; God as Immanuel. As we explore these themes, we will observe both continuity between the Old and New Testaments and discontinuity as Jesus Christ radically fulfils what the Old Testament anticipates.

The Establishment of Covenant between Yahweh and His People

Wherever in the Old Testament we might be reading, we are likely to encounter the concept of covenant. In the first place, there are frequent scenes where God makes a covenant with his people. We see this for the first time with Noah (Gen. 9).[5] Next we note that Abraham enjoys a covenant relationship with God. Nowhere do we see God actually entering into a covenant relationship with Abraham, but certainly the promises of Genesis 12:1–3 presuppose it. Exodus 19–24 is the heart of the description of the covenant made between God and Israel on Mount Sinai. Moses was the mediator between the two parties who entered into this relationship. Later God also made a covenant with David (2 Sam. 7; 1 Chron. 17).

Besides the scenes of covenant making, there are passages in which the various covenants are renewed. No new terms are initiated; there are no new promises or responsibilities. Rather, the already existent relationship is reaffirmed. A few examples will suffice to show that renewals frequently come at times of uncertainty or crisis, such as a transition from one leader to another. Genesis 15 and 17 recount two separate incidents when God comes to Abraham to reaffirm his promise of numerous descendants. To become "the father of a great nation" (Gen. 12:2) Abraham first of all needs a son. But as he gets older, he begins to doubt the possibility of having a child with the aging Sarah. Thus twice he utilizes human conventions to attain an heir. In Genesis 15 he alludes to his adopting Eliezer his household servant. In Genesis 16 he has a child through Hagar his concubine. Both times God appears to Abraham and graciously reaffirms the covenant with him.

The whole Book of Deuteronomy is a reaffirmation of the covenant that God made with Israel at Sinai. The crisis that necessitated the renewal was the impending death of Moses. Indeed, the next reaffirmation, also of the Mosaic covenant, is recorded in Joshua 24, just before the death of Joshua. But there is also a hint in the Book of Deuteronomy that the covenant was reaffirmed at periodic intervals whether there was a crisis or not:

> So Moses wrote down this law and gave it to the priests, who carried the Ark of the LORD's covenant, and to the leaders of Israel. Then Moses gave them this command: "At the end of every seventh year, the Year of Release, during the Festival of Shelters, you must read this law to all the people of Israel when they assemble before the LORD your God at the place he chooses. Call them all together—men, women, children, and the foreigners living in your towns—so they may listen and learn to fear the LORD your

God and carefully obey all the terms of this law. Do this so that
your children who have not known these laws will hear them and
will learn to fear the LORD your God. Do this as long as you live
in the land you are crossing the Jordan to occupy." [Deut.
31:9–13]

Covenant as Metaphorical Relationship

The numerous references to covenant making and renewal
establish the covenant idea as a major biblical concept. But do
we really understand what it means? Let's explore the nature of
covenant and then see how it provides continuity between the
Old and New Testament understandings of God.

The first thing to note is that covenant is a metaphorical relationship. The English word "covenant," which translates the
Hebrew term *běrît*, is an old legal term. Indeed, it is only in legal
language that one finds this word outside of the Bible. A covenant
is a legally binding agreement between two parties. Although this
term is inadequate to explain the biblical concept, it does show
us that we are dealing with a legal relationship between God and
humanity.

Covenant as Treaty

By setting the concept in its historical and cultural context
(see pp. 47–48), we can be much more precise in our understanding of covenant in the Old Testament. Not that we have
misunderstood the covenant for years; we have not. But view-
ing the biblical covenants as treaties does allow us a richer and
more profound appreciation of the force of the concept. It also
provides a better foundation for appropriating the concept into
our present-day understanding of the nature of God and our
relationship with him.

In the middle of the twentieth century, research revealed a
close literary connection between the biblical covenants and
ancient Near Eastern political treaties. Most of these treaties,

written in Akkadian, come from either the second millennium (the Hittite treaties) or the neo-Assyrian period (seventh century B.C.).[6] Differences between the two groups were used by some scholars in attempts to resolve issues of dating (in particular, the writing of Deuteronomy). However, the differences are neither pronounced nor consistent enough to provide conclusive evidence.

Another distinction, however, that between parity treaties and vassal treaties, has proved helpful in our understanding of biblical covenants. The former are treaties between kings of nations with near equal power. A contemporary example would be a treaty between the United States and China. One such ancient treaty involved Egypt and Hatti, an Anatolian power during the mid-second millennium. On the other hand, a vassal treaty is an alliance between a great king and a lesser king. A good example today might be a treaty between the United States and Haiti. An ancient example is a treaty between Hatti and Ugarit, a small city-state on the Mediterranean coast just below what is today Turkey.

The vassal treaties are substantially different in tone and structure from the parity treaties. After all, what we have in a vassal treaty is the imposition of the will of a powerful king upon that of a lesser king. That the balance of power is so one-sided in a vassal treaty makes it a better pattern for the biblical covenants. For in the biblical covenants the powerful king Yahweh enters into relationship with his creatures, his vassals. By the way, this is the heart of the metaphor of the covenant: Yahweh the king is bound by treaty to his people.

The Structure of the Covenant/Treaty

God, then, used a human legal convention, the treaty, to reveal himself to his people. The treaty also enriched their understanding of who they were as the people of God. The close connection between these biblical covenants and international treaties is reflected in their similar structures, which typically consist of six basic parts. For our biblical examples we will use the Book of Deuteronomy and Joshua 24, both of which were renewals of the Mosaic covenant. (Since the Bible presents descriptions of covenant making and renewal rather than the documents themselves, our analogy will have some fuzzy edges. But even so the similarities are striking.)

1. INTRODUCTION OF THE PARTIES

The first part of a treaty simply introduced the two parties entering into the relationship. The great king and the lesser king are both mentioned by name. The opening of Deuteronomy (1:1–5) informs the reader that the people of Israel are listening to the words of Moses, the representative of God. In Joshua 24 the people stand before Joshua, who likewise serves as the representative of the Lord. The text here goes as far as to say that the people "presented themselves to God" (v. 1). The parties are present and ready to hear the words of the covenant/treaty.

2. HISTORICAL PROLOGUE

After the introduction the vassal treaties then recount the history of the relationship between the two nations up to the present moment. The emphasis is on how gracious and helpful the great king has been toward the vassal king. Now in the political treaties of the ancient Near East this likely involved just so much political propaganda as the powerful king couched what was likely a history of oppression and exploitation in the language of love and care for the vassal. God, however, devoided the form of its hypocrisy, recounting the history in a way that showed how gracious and loving Yahweh had been toward his people. We can see this in a large section of Deuteronomy (1:9–3:27) and also in Joshua 24:2–13. In the latter, the history begins with Abraham and his family before entering the Promised Land and climaxes with the moment at which Israel stands in the Promised Land as a great nation. Joshua, speaking on behalf of God, recounts the crossing of the Red Sea, the conquest and possession of the land, and much more.

3. LAW

Having engendered a sense of gratitude and responsibility in the vassal, the historical recital leads directly into the giving of the law, which will henceforth regulate the relationship. The purpose of the historical report is to lay a burden of responsibility on the vassal, and then the law, which seems to be the center of the treaty, is the great king's attempt to give concrete shape to the vassal's grateful response.

In the political treaties the law often has to do with the responsibility of the vassal king to support the great king's foreign policy, to make his enemies their enemies, to make his friends their friends. In the biblical texts the transition from history to law is seen as a movement from the past to the present and is marked by the adverb "now" (or "so"; the Hebrew is 'attâ). We see such a transition in Joshua 24:14 as we move from the historical recital, which ends in verse 13, to the imperatives of law: "So honor the LORD and serve him wholeheartedly. Put away forever the idols your ancestors worshiped when they lived beyond the Euphrates River and in Egypt. Serve the LORD alone." In Deuteronomy the section of law is much longer; indeed, it dominates the book (Deut. 4:1–26:19).

The basically legal nature of a covenant/treaty has been recognized by all scholars and explains the choice of "covenant" or "testament," both legal terms, to translate the Hebrew *bĕrît* and the Greek *diathēkē* into English. However, we must be careful to guard against a very dangerous distortion of the legal nature of covenants. A covenant/treaty did not establish a relationship that was based on the observation of law, though it did enforce it. The great king had already conquered or cowed the other king into vassalage by the time the treaty was written. In the case of the Mosaic covenant, God had already established his relationship with Israel by means of his grace before giving them the law. Indeed, the preface to the Ten Commandments indicates as much when God introduces himself as the one "who rescued you from slavery in Egypt" (Exod. 20:1).

4. BLESSINGS AND CURSES

Being a legal document, it is not surprising that the covenant/ treaty contains blessings and curses that follow on the heels of the law. If the vassal king follows the laws, then the great king will reward him with peace, wealth, prosperity, and secure dynastic succession. Most importantly, the great king will protect the vassal from external enemies. However, if the vassal rebels against the great king, then the vassal will feel the anger of the great king, who will move militarily against the vassal, bringing him under control and punishing him for his rebellion.

By now we are not surprised to see that the biblical covenants follow the pattern of the political treaties. Joshua 24 emphasizes the curses: "If you forsake the LORD and serve other gods, he will turn against you and destroy you, even though he has been so good to you" (24:20). The longer covenant renewal in Deuteronomy contains extensive blessings (28:1–14) and curses (27:11–26; 28:15–68). Indeed, these blessings and curses drive much of what follows in the rest of the Old Testament canon. Historical books like Joshua, Judges, Samuel, and Kings show how the curses of Deuteronomy continue to follow rebellious Israel. In addition, the prophets often base their speeches of judgment on these curses.

5. WITNESSES

Like most legal documents, the treaty was ratified in the presence of witnesses. In the ancient Near Eastern treaties, the gods and goddesses of the respective nations often served in this capacity. For Israel, the witnesses could be the Israelites themselves (Josh. 24:22), a monument that would be erected as a reminder of the terms of the covenant (Josh. 24:26), or God's creation, heaven and earth (Deut. 30:19–20).

6. REVIEW AND SUCCESSION

To complete the picture of the treaty or covenant in Old Testament times, we must mention the concern for the safekeeping and regular reading of the document, as well as the provision for the succession of kings, especially in the vassal country. Treaties looked beyond the present to the future. So scribes made two copies of the treaty and usually placed them in the most important temples of the two nations entering the relationship. This procedure wasn't necessary in the biblical divine-human covenant, though it has been suggested that the two tablets of the law are actually two copies. Whatever the case, the law was written and placed in the most sacred spot possible—the ark of the covenant. Every seven years, during the Feast of Tabernacles of the jubilee year, the priests would read the law so the people could reaffirm their allegiance to it (Deut. 31:9–13).

It is hard to avoid the conclusion that the Old Testament covenant is a treaty between the great king, Yahweh, and his vassal, his servant people. The covenant is, accordingly, a relational metaphor highlighting the fact that God is Israel's king. It therefore fits in quite well with many passages in the Bible that have a royal theme.[7]

Jesus Christ and Fulfilment of the Covenant

But the question at hand is how the Old Testament conception of God fits with the New. Is there discontinuity or continuity? As we focus on the theme of God as our covenant king, the answer is—both.

At the end of his life, just before going to the cross, Jesus shared a last meal with his disciples. At this meal he introduced a ritual which we know as the Lord's Supper or communion:

As they were eating, Jesus took a loaf of bread and asked God's blessing on it. Then he broke it in pieces and gave it to the disciples, saying, "Take it and eat it, for this is my body." And he took a cup of wine and gave thanks to God for it. He gave it to them and said, "Each of you drink from it, for this is my blood, which seals the covenant between God and his people. It is poured out to forgive the sins of many. Mark my words—I will not drink wine again until the day I drink it new with you in my Father's Kingdom." Then they sang a hymn and went out to the Mount of Olives. [Matt. 26:26–30]

Jesus thus sealed with his disciples a covenant that reminds us of God's covenant dealings in the Old Testament. As a matter of fact, Luke adds the word "new" before covenant (22:20), making an explicit connection with Jeremiah 31:31–33. Jesus' language signifies continuity and discontinuity as we move from the Old to the New Testament, a transition in which Jeremiah's prophecy plays a crucial role.

Jeremiah was a prophet at the end of the seventh and beginning of the sixth centuries B.C. Israel had a long history of covenant relationship with God, but also a long history of not obeying the law of the covenant. As a result, Jeremiah was commissioned by God to tell them that the curses of the covenant were about to go into effect so that they would end up in exile (Deut. 28:63–68).

But God did not leave Israel without hope. He also instructed Jeremiah to tell his people that his punishment would lead to their repentance and to the rescue of a remnant. The most notable instance of this promise is found in the so-called book of consolation, where Jeremiah 31:31–34 is at the heart of God's message of hope:

> "The day will come," says the LORD, "when I will make a new covenant with the people of Israel and Judah. This covenant will not be like the one I made with their ancestors when I took them

by the hand and brought them out of the land of Egypt. They
broke that covenant, though I loved them as a husband loves his
wife," says the LORD.

"But this is the new covenant I will make with the people of
Israel on that day," says the LORD. "I will put my laws in their
minds, and I will write them on their hearts. I will be their God,
and they will be my people. And they will not need to teach
their neighbors, nor will they need to teach their family, saying,
'You should know the LORD.' For everyone, from the least to
the greatest, will already know me," says the LORD. "And I will
forgive their wickedness and will never again remember their
sins."

Here we see a bridge between the Old Testament and the New,
one that suggests both continuity and discontinuity. It is a
covenant which has its foundations in the Old Testament
covenants, but is in some sense new. Let's explore what is new
in the new covenant, that is to say, the discontinuity between the
old and the new. We should note at the start that Palmer Robertson is correct to locate the necessity of discontinuity not in any
failure on God's part or in the covenant, but with the people:
"The expulsion of the people of God from the land of promise
at the time of the exile dramatizes their massive failure under
the old covenant."[8]

According to Jeremiah, the new covenant when compared to
the old covenant is internal, immediate, and intimate. These differences are not differences in kind so much as degree. It is perhaps more precise to say that the new covenant is more internal, immediate, and intimate than the old. Jeremiah 31 attributes
to the new covenant "a unique feature in its power to transform
its participants from within their hearts."[9] Further, there is no
need for a teacher in the new covenant. Now Christians know
by experience that the new covenant does not imply that we
know everything or that everything concerning God and his
Word is clear to us. It also does not mean that teachers and min-

isters should seek employment elsewhere. What it does mean is that human mediators of the covenant relationship are no longer needed. In the Old Testament, Moses, David, and various other leaders were the immediate recipients of the covenant relationship; and they mediated it to the people. According to the New Testament, there is only one mediator; he is not merely human, but Jesus Christ, Son of God (1 Tim. 2:5).

On the other hand, the word "new" does not imply a complete break with the old. Recognizing this, Robertson calls the new covenant the covenant of consummation. This highlights the fact that Jesus Christ does not abrogate or ignore the old covenants but fulfils them. Robertson utilizes what his former students used to call the "lazy V" diagram to indicate that the covenants are a function of progressive revelation, each building on the previous

Figure 1
The Covenantal Structure of Scripture

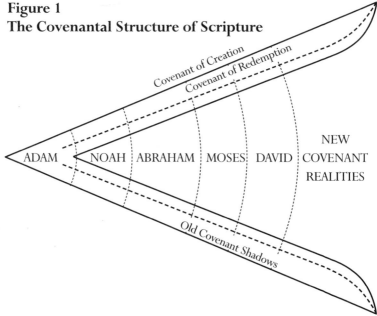

From O. Palmer Robertson, *The Christ of the Covenants* (Grand Rapids: Baker, 1980), 62.

ones until they are all consummated in Christ (see figure 1). Jesus fulfils the covenant with Abraham with its promises of descendants, land, and blessing for the nations. Jesus fulfils the covenant of law mediated by Moses, since he is the one who fulfils the conditions of the law. He also fulfils the covenant of the kingdom of David, since he is David's greater Son who sits on the throne of the heavenly kingdom adumbrated by David's political kingdom.

We have seen that covenant is a leading metaphor of the Bible, arguably the most pervasive biblical image of the relationship between God and his people. As we follow the trajectory of this concept from the Old to the New Testament, we see that there is neither simple identity nor blunt contrast between the covenants. The new covenant of Jesus Christ is certainly different from the old covenants, but it is not as if the former replaces the latter. Rather, the covenant king of the New Testament is the fulfilment that is anticipated in the Old. The God of the New Testament is clearly the same as the God of the Old Testament; the difference is that we have come to know him better.

The Metaphor of the Divine Warrior

When we explore the theology of God as a warrior,[10] we are at the heart of many people's suspicion that the Old and New Testaments offer different and even contradictory pictures of God. The vengeful, violent Yahweh is placed over against the loving, compassionate Jesus. But as we examine the theme of God as warrior throughout the whole of Scripture, we will, as we did with the concept of covenant, observe that, while there is indeed discontinuity, there is also strong continuity as we move from the holy wars of Yahweh to the spiritual warfare of Jesus and then finally to the climactic battles associated with the second coming of Christ and the final judgment. Once again we will see a pattern of ever-fuller revelation.

Holy War in the Old Testament

As we read through the pages of the Old Testament, we encounter many violent scenes. From Abraham's battle to free Lot from raiding kings (Gen. 14) through the conquest of Canaan to the postexilic period, we read of many wars and armed struggles. As we turn to the crucial and influential law code in Deuteronomy, we also find almost two whole chapters (7 and 20) devoted to laws which regulated warfare for the people of God. It is from these laws as well as the historical descriptions that we derive our synthesis of warfare in the Old Testament.

BEFORE A BATTLE

Discerning the will of God. God promised to protect Israel, his chosen people. However, that did not mean that Israel could battle whomever they wanted in whatever way they chose. For one thing, the law (see Deut. 20:10–18) made a clear distinction between enemy towns that were outside and enemy towns that were inside the Promised Land. While the former could surrender and be subjected to slavery, the entire population of the latter was to be executed.

But there is more. Israel had to know in some concrete way that God wanted them to war against a specific enemy at a specific time. This could happen in one of two ways: divine command or oracular inquiry. Illustrative of the first is the battle of Jericho. After crossing the Jordan River, Joshua was reconnoitering when he encountered a strange figure with a drawn sword (Josh. 5:13–15). In response to Joshua's challenge, the figure identified himself as the "commander of the LORD's army." Joshua's taking off his sandals and bowing in an act of obeisance similar to what Moses did at the burning bush (Exod. 3) make it clear that this figure was none other than Yahweh himself. As we read the battle account in the next chapter, we realize that Yahweh at this time both commissioned and imparted war strategy to Joshua.

An example of the second type of commissioning, oracular inquiry, is found in 1 Samuel 23. This passage describes David's flight from a furious King Saul. Even though he is not yet king, David has all the trappings of royalty. He has a standing army, a prophet, and a priest in attendance. So when David hears that the Judean city of Keilah is under attack by Philistines, he wonders whether he should go to its rescue. David does not go impulsively, however. He summons the priest-in-exile Abiathar and asks him to use the ephod to inquire of God. God gives an affirmative answer, and David sets off on his divinely appointed task.

We have one occasion on record when the war leader failed to consult God. The time is the conquest, and Joshua's troops have with divine aid just been victorious over the mighty town of Jericho. They have struggled with Ai but in the end prevailed. Now they are approached by a motley, apparently travel-weary group who represent themselves as having come some distance (Josh. 9). Joshua, understanding the distinction between cities within and outside of the Promised Land, agrees to enter into an alliance with these people, whom we know to be Gibeonites. Soon after this, Joshua realizes his mistake. They have tricked him; they are actually a tribe from the interior of the land. The fault here lies with the Israelite leaders, for, according to Joshua 9:14, they "examined [the Gibeonites'] bread, but they did not consult the LORD."

Spiritual preparation. In addition to discerning the will of God, it was of crucial importance that the Israelites be spiritually prepared before going into battle. Before the battle of Jericho, for instance, Israel observed the Passover and—strikingly—all the males were circumcised. For some unstated reason, the Israelites born in the wilderness had not been circumcised, so before proceeding to the first battle of the conquest it was mandatory to do so. The urgency of the act can be seen in the military disadvantage it obviously placed on the Israelites. They were, after all, within striking distance of their enemy. The act of circumcision rendered the Israelite fighters temporarily impaired (compare the account of the slaughter of Shechem in Gen. 34). But it was apparently more dangerous for the Israelites to go to battle spiritually (cultically) unprepared than for them to be physically disadvantaged. Another indication of the necessity of spiritual preparation is the prebattle sacrifices. Consider, for example, 1 Samuel 13, a story in which the battle preparations go awry. As the newly appointed king, Saul's main task was to rid the Israelites of their oppressors, namely, the Philistines. The Philistines were moving toward the heart of Saul's kingdom with a mighty army. Saul was obviously nervous, and so were the troops, some of them to the point of deserting. Saul thought that unless he moved fast, all his troops would soon be hiding in the hills. Yet he could not go to battle without offering sacrifice to God, and Samuel the priest was nowhere to be found. Saul then panicked and offered the sacrifices himself.

It is significant that Saul did not simply skip the sacrifices. They were absolutely critical. However, when Samuel arrived, he expressed God's anger at the king's presumption in offering the sacrifices himself. After all, Saul was not a priest; he had overstepped his limits. As a result, God removed from him any hope that he would establish a dynasty in Israel. His sin was likely his lack of trust in God the warrior to protect him until Samuel showed up.

We will cite one more narrative from the Old Testament in connection with spiritual preparation for battle. Second Samuel 11 contains the famous scene where David and Uriah face each other after the king has impregnated Bathsheba, Uriah's wife. David is attempting to cover up his adultery by calling Uriah back from the front lines, where he has been serving under Joab in the war against the Ammonites. After receiving Uriah's report, David sends him home. The next day David is distressed on learning that, instead of sleeping with Bathsheba, Uriah has slept at the palace entrance. Foiled in his intention, David demands, "What's the matter with you? Why didn't you go home last night after being away for so long?" (11:10). Uriah's response seems, at first, enigmatic: "The Ark and the armies of Israel and Judah are living in tents, and Joab and his officers are camping in the open fields. How could I go home to wine and dine and sleep with my wife? I swear that I will never be guilty of acting like that" (11:11).

A modern reader might interpret Uriah's response to say, in effect, "How can I enjoy myself and relax when my comrades are risking their lives?" While Uriah's response may have a bit of that in mind, the mention of the ark tips us off that there are grander, more theological issues at stake here. If Uriah had gone home and slept with his wife, he would have fallen under the provision of the law of Leviticus 15:1–18: a man who has an emission of semen, even in the context of marital intercourse, is ritually unclean for twenty-four hours and cannot approach God. In that condition Uriah could not have gone back to the battlefield.

It is noteworthy that the narrative puts Uriah in a good light at the expense of David. Uriah is not even an Israelite; he is a Hittite mercenary who apparently has turned to the Lord. He shows himself fastidious to the details of the law. David, on the other hand, is not only an Israelite, but also God's favorite and the king. He is futilely trying to cover up his breaking of the seventh commandment and soon will resort to murder.

The ark. Few would contest the statement that the ark was the most potent symbol of the presence of God in the Old Testament.[11] It occupied the central place in the tabernacle's Holy of Holies. Its mobility also made it ideal to represent God on the battlefield.

Perhaps the most well known episode in which the ark plays a major role is the battle of Jericho. The Lord instructed Joshua: "Your entire army is to march around the city once a day for six days. Seven priests will walk ahead of the Ark, each carrying a ram's horn. On the seventh day you are to march around the city seven times, with the priests blowing the horns. When you hear the priests give one long blast on the horns, have all the people give a mighty shout. Then the walls of the city will collapse, and the people can charge straight into the city" (Josh. 6:3–5). The centrality of the ark in this narrative emphasizes God's pivotal role in the battle: it is God who causes the walls to crumble.

Before Jericho, the ark also had an important place in the wilderness wanderings. The words spoken before and after a day's march clearly demonstrate that it was conceived of as a military procedure and that God was viewed as a war leader: "Whenever the Ark set out, Moses would cry, 'Arise, O LORD, and let your enemies be scattered! Let them flee before you!' And when the Ark was set down, he would say, 'Return, O LORD, to the countless thousands of Israel!'" (Num. 10:35–36). The ark's presence at the head of the march parallels the role of a king who personally leads his army. Thus we are not surprised that the ark, like the king's tent, is placed in the middle of the camp when the Israelites are at rest (Num. 2).

The march. During the days of the conquest of Canaan, the ark represented Yahweh as the army of Israel went on the march. Similarly, the account of the march of Jehoshaphat's army into battle in 2 Chronicles 20 is indicative of the religious nature of warfare in the Old Testament:

> Early the next morning the army of Judah went out into the wilderness of Tekoa. On the way Jehoshaphat stopped and said, "Listen to me, all you people of Judah and Jerusalem! Believe in the LORD your God, and you will be able to stand firm. Believe in his prophets, and you will succeed." After consulting the leaders of the people, the king appointed singers to walk ahead of the army, singing to the LORD and praising him for his holy splendor. This is what they sang:

> "Give thanks to the LORD;
>   his faithful love endures forever!" [vv. 20–21]

During a Battle

A remarkable characteristic of Old Testament warfare is the disregard of the number of troops and even of the quality of weapons used in a battle. Perhaps "disregard" is the wrong word; God was concerned about the number of troops Israel took into a battle. He was concerned that they not have too many troops. The story of Gideon illustrates this concern well. Observing that thirty-two thousand troops have massed against the Midianites, God informs Gideon, "You have too many warriors with you" (Judg. 7:2). When those who are afraid are allowed to leave, twenty-two thousand go home. But ten thousand is still too many. God then orders the troops to drink from the wadi Harod. The three hundred who cup the water in their hands and lap it up with their tongues are chosen to fight. Much ink has been spilled on the question why God chose these soldiers. What was so special about this mode of drinking? The answer is, nothing. God just did not want Israel to have too many troops for fear that they would "boast to me that they saved themselves by their own strength" (7:2b).

The fight between David and Goliath illustrates this concern on the level of individual combat. The Philistines suggested to the Israelites that they settle their conflict by means of a fight of champions.[12] The Philistines likely felt that they had nothing to lose considering that they had Goliath on their side. He was huge and armed to the teeth with the latest in weapon technology (1 Sam. 17:4–7). On the other hand, the Israelites had only the lad David, who was unable to wear armor and was equipped with only a slingshot. This mismatch ended with David's victory, not because of his skill but because of God's presence on his side.

After the War

If the war was a holy war, there was no doubt about the outcome. Israel was the winner. If the battle was within the Promised

Land, God's command was clear. All the booty would be "devoted" to God (the meaning of the Hebrew term *ḥerem*). This meant that the valuables would be turned over to the priests and that all survivors would be executed. This was the fate of sinners who go into the presence of God without being covered by sacrifices.[13]

Since God had won the victory, Israel's proper response was not to celebrate their strength but God's. A number of songs in the historical books (e.g., Exod. 15 and Judg. 5) are good examples. Many psalms likewise arose from a warfare setting, particularly in the context of a victory (see Pss. 24 and 98). Thus after the battle, just as before and during, the focus of the Israelites was on God.[14]

A Biblical Theology of Divine Warfare

In our survey of holy war in the Old Testament the overarching principle is that Yahweh is present in the battle. Thus warfare is actually a form of worship. That is why, for instance, it is necessary for the Israelite warrior to be in a state of spiritual preparedness. It is as if he is walking into the temple precincts.

No one states the theology of holy war better than does the young David as he faces the giant Goliath. Just before they join battle, David triumphantly declares:

> You come to me with sword, spear, and javelin, but I come to you in the name of the LORD Almighty—the God of the armies of Israel, whom you have defied. Today the LORD will conquer you, and I will kill you and cut off your head. And then I will give the dead bodies of your men to the birds and wild animals, and the whole world will know that there is a God in Israel! And everyone will know that the LORD does not need weapons to rescue his people. It is his battle, not ours. The LORD will give you to us!" [1 Sam. 17:45–47]

In the Old Testament, Yahweh fights on behalf of his people. As we broaden our study to include the development of redemptive history, we will observe that there is a progressive pattern to God's warring activity. We will look at five distinct phases of divine warfare in the Bible. Though not strictly sequential, they do reflect the development of the history of redemption (see figure 2).

Figure 2
The Phases of Divine Warfare

		Christ's First Coming	Christ's Second Coming
Phase 1 God's fight against the flesh-and-blood enemies of Israel	**Phase 3** Postexilic anticipation of the divine warrior	**Phase 4** Jesus Christ's fight against Satan	**Phase 5** The final battle
Phase 2 God's fight against Israel			

1. GOD'S FIGHT AGAINST THE FLESH-AND-BLOOD ENEMIES OF ISRAEL

Our description of holy war in the Old Testament was really a description of the first phase of divine warfare. God fights against Israel's flesh-and-blood enemies and brings his people the victory. He does not, however, war for Israel indiscriminately. His fighting is connected to his covenant promise to protect them when they are obedient to him (Deut. 28:7).

The first explicit mention of God as a warrior appears in Exodus 15. After God had won the victory over the Egyptian army at the Red Sea, Moses and the people responded by singing:

> The LORD is my strength and my song;
>   he has become my victory.
> He is my God, and I will praise him;
>   he is my father's God, and I will exalt him!
> The LORD is a warrior;
>   yes, the LORD is his name! [vv. 2–3]

Even though Exodus 15 is the first explicit mention of Yahweh as warrior, his military nature was earlier revealed when he declared war on the serpent for having seduced his image bearers to sin: "From now on, you and the woman will be enemies, and your offspring and her offspring will be enemies. He will crush your head, and you will strike his heel" (Gen. 3:15).

Many of the wars of the Old Testament fall into this first category. To mention just a few besides the Red Sea conflict, we may think of the wars of conquest, the conflicts of the judges against Israel's oppressors, David's wars against the Philistines, and Nahum's prophecy of the destruction of Nineveh.

2. GOD'S FIGHT AGAINST ISRAEL

The covenant not only promised victory for Israel's obedience, but also threatened defeat for disobedience. For instance, Deuteronomy 28:25–26 warns, "The LORD will cause you to be defeated by your enemies. You will attack your enemies from one direction, but you will scatter from them in seven! You will be an object of horror to all the kingdoms of the earth. Your dead bodies will be food for the birds and wild animals, and no one will be there to chase them away." Unfortunately, these threats were frequently carried out, for Israel did not remain consistently faithful to the Lord, their divine warrior.

As Jericho was the paradigm of victory in return for Israel's obedience, so Ai, the very next battle, was the paradigm of the consequences of disobedience. While Jericho was the oldest, probably richest, and most well defended city in the Promised Land, Ai was a city of no real reputation. Indeed, its very name means "ruin," so Joshua did not take it seriously, sending only a relatively small detachment of troops to take the city. However, unknown to Joshua, a man named Achan had infringed on the principles of ḥerem warfare by keeping some of the wealth of Jericho for himself. As a result, the Israelites were defeated at Ai until this situation was taken care of.

It is no accident that the battles of Jericho and Ai are narrated at much greater length than are the battles with other cities. These reports are more than historical records or even historical-theological tracts; they are also didactic texts, instructing later generations about the results of obedience ("If you cling to God, he will bring you victory no matter how great the enemy") and of disobedience ("God will cause even a weak enemy to send you running").

Certainly the most fearsome illustration of reverse holy war is the Babylonian conquest and exile.[15] While the Israelites presumed on God's presence in Jerusalem to rescue them (Jer. 7), God abandoned the city (Ezek. 9–11). Not only did he allow the city to be destroyed by the Babylonians, he took an active part in the defeat (Jer. 21:3–7). Nowhere is the anguish of this devastating defeat expressed more poignantly than in the Book of Lamentations, where God is pictured as Israel's enemy:

> He bends his bow against his people as though he were their enemy. His strength is used against them to kill their finest youth. His fury is poured out like fire on beautiful Jerusalem.
>
> Yes, the Lord has vanquished Israel like an enemy. He has destroyed her forts and palaces. He has brought unending sorrow and tears to Jerusalem. [2:4–5]

3. Postexilic Anticipation of the Divine Warrior

The Babylonian exile could have easily been the end of Israel's story. The people of God had systematically and consciously rejected God. They presumed on his faithfulness while they wantonly disobeyed him. However, as with Adam and Eve after the fall, God did not utterly abandon his creatures.

Throughout the exile and into the postexilic period God commissioned prophets to bring a message of hope in the midst of oppression. Of course, the preexilic prophets had anticipated some type of restoration: a message of hope (see, e.g., Jer. 30–31) was embedded within their threats of judgment. But the exilic and postexilic prophets assumed that the people of God would continue after the exile, though still under oppression. From our vantage point we know that after the Israelites returned to their homeland pursuant to Cyrus's decree in 538 B.C., they lived under the respective oppressions of Persia, Greece, and Rome.[16]

Zechariah 14 is an example of a postexilic prophecy of hope in the midst of present suffering. It begins with a warning to anticipate the coming "day of the LORD": "Watch, for the day of the LORD is coming when your possessions will be plundered right in front of you! On that day I will gather all the nations to fight against Jerusalem. The city will be taken, the houses plundered, and the women raped. Half the population will be taken away into captivity, and half will be left among the ruins of the city" (14:1–2). But just when the situation looks most bleak, Zechariah goes on to say, "Then the LORD will go out to fight against those nations, as he has fought in times past" (14:3). The following verses describe the cataclysmic consequences of the appearance of God the warrior. There will be earthquakes, the heavenly army will come, daylight will turn to darkness, rivers will flow from Jerusalem. Plagues and destruction will ensue. The ultimate result will be victory for the Lord and worldwide worship of him as king. The whole world will be dedicated to him (14:20–21).

This is the note on which the Old Testament comes to an end. The people of God look to the future and eagerly expect the appearance of the divine warrior who will free them from oppression.

4. Jesus Christ's Fight against Satan

The fiery words of John the Baptist bring to mind the Old Testament expectation of a future divine warrior:

> Even now the ax of God's judgment is poised ready to sever your roots. Yes, every tree that does not produce good fruit will be chopped down and thrown into the fire. I baptize with water those who turn from their sins and turn to God. But someone

is coming soon who is far greater than I am—so much greater
that I am not even worthy to be his slave. He will baptize you
with the Holy Spirit and with fire. He is ready to separate the
chaff from the grain with his winnowing fork. Then he will clean
up the threshing area, storing the grain in his barn but burning
the chaff with never-ending fire. [Matt. 3:10–12]

When Jesus comes to the Jordan, John recognizes him as the one
who is expected and baptizes him. At this point John's ministry
decreases while that of Jesus increases. John is arrested by Herod
and thrown into jail.

While he is in jail, John begins to hear disturbing reports that
lead him to question whether he baptized the wrong individual.
So he sends two of his disciples to Jesus with this question, "Are
you really the Messiah we've been waiting for, or should we keep
looking for someone else?" (Matt. 11:3). What is going on in
John's mind? He is the forerunner of the Messiah, the future
divine warrior, whom he expects to lead a violent physical battle
against the enemies of the people of God. Jesus, however, has
undermined John's expectations by healing the sick, exorcising
demons, and preaching the Good News. Indeed, Jesus responds
to John's disciples by doing more preaching and performing more
healings and exorcisms.

What is Jesus saying by these actions? Jesus is saying, "John,
you were right. I am the Messiah, the coming warrior. But the
warfare that I have come to wage is more intense, more dangerous than the physical battles that you expect. I have come to
bring the fight against Satan himself." This is how the exorcisms
should be understood. They are part of the spiritual battle that
Jesus wages against the powers and principalities.

Among the changes wrought by the coming of Jesus is not only
the primary object of warfare but the weapons used. In the Old
Testament, human soldiers used physical weapons: swords, javelins,
spears, bows and arrows. God even used weapons like hailstones.

But when Jesus is arrested, he shows the radical nature of the transition by saying to Peter, "Put away your sword" (Matt. 26:52). And then he goes to the cross, where he wins the battle against Satan not by killing, but by dying. Paul understands this act on the cross as a great military victory: "[God] canceled the record that contained the charges against us. He took it and destroyed it by nailing it to Christ's cross. In this way, God disarmed the evil rulers and authorities. He shamed them publicly by his victory over them on the cross of Christ" (Col. 2:14–15).

We can see here the continuity and discontinuity between the Old and New Testaments. Jesus is the divine warrior, but he wages his warfare in a heightened and intensified manner against the spiritual powers which stand behind all evil in the world. While passages like Daniel 10 in the Old Testament indicate that there is a spiritual struggle going on behind the scenes, the New Testament gives us a much clearer grasp of the situation. However, even with Jesus' victory on the cross, we are not at the end of the story.

5. The Final Battle

It is when we come to the fifth and final phase of the Bible's unfolding drama of divine warfare that we see that John the Baptist was not wrong. To be more precise, he was a typical human prophet in that he spoke God's words better than he knew. It has long been noted that the prophets often spoke of coming events as if they were going to happen at a discrete moment in time, but that the subsequent fulfilment actually unfolded over time. This is true of Jesus' appearance as a warrior. Jesus' coming was not a one-time event; he came once in our past, and he is coming again in our future.

Jesus himself told his disciples to expect him to come again. In doing so, he used a highly charged metaphor to describe his return: "Everyone will see the Son of Man arrive on the clouds with great power and glory" (Mark 13:26). The Book of Revelation picks up this image: "Look! He comes with the clouds of heaven. And everyone will see him—even those who pierced him. And all the nations of the earth will weep because of him. Yes! Amen!" (Rev. 1:7).

In the Old Testament, Yahweh rides a cloud into battle. That a cloud is the war chariot of the divine warrior is a theme in the Psalms (18:9–10; 68:33; 104:3) and the prophets (Nah. 1:3). The New Testament passages regarding Jesus, however, are more immediately linked to Daniel 7:13. The context is Daniel's end-of-the-Old-Testament prediction of the divine warrior's future invasion to rid the world of evil. The second coming of Christ is seen in the New Testament as the ultimate fulfilment of this expectation. Jesus is coming again to finish off the victory that he has won on the cross.

Many passages in the Book of Revelation develop the theme of Jesus' triumphant return, but we will cite only one, Revelation 19:11–21. Here another metaphor is used for Jesus' return. This time he is envisioned as riding a white horse at the head of the heavenly army. A sword is coming out of his mouth, and he is "clothed with a robe dipped in blood." This quotation comes from Isaiah 63:3, where Yahweh the divine warrior is described.

The apocalyptic passages of the New Testament thus bring to a dramatic conclusion the unfolding story of God's warfare. This story began at the fall, specifically with the curse on the serpent in Genesis 3:15, and ends with the casting of Satan into the pit. At this time the human and spiritual enemies of God will be judged. Death and the grave will be destroyed (Rev. 20:11–15), and a "new heaven and earth" will come into existence (Rev. 21–22).

A superficial reading of the Bible, as we have seen, would pit the violence of the God of the Old Testament over against the kindness of Jesus Christ. While a closer reading does not completely abrogate this distinction, it does reveal that the New Testament is a fulfilment in continuity with the Old Testament and not a replacement of the teaching found there. As we read of the fights of the Israelites giving way to the spiritual battles of the church, which in turn anticipate the final battle at the end of time, we see God's progressive plan in motion.

The Metaphor of Immanuel: God's Presence with His People

A third theme which illustrates the continuity and discontinuity between the presentation of God in the Old and New Testaments is the Immanuel metaphor. The Hebrew word "Immanuel," which literally means "God is with us," denotes the presence of God with his people. This theme is another area where some readers of the Bible think they see a contrast between the Testaments. In the Old Testament, they say, God seems distant, while in the New Testament, God draws close to his people. We will see that there is some truth to this impression, but the contrast does not imply a contradiction. As we trace the development of God's plan of redemption from Genesis to Revelation, we will see that, as with the theme of the divine warrior, there are a number of distinct phases (see figure 3).

The Garden of Eden

Before the Fall

After Adam was created, he was placed in the Garden of Eden (Gen. 2:8), where Eve was then created. Thus the Garden was the first home of humanity. The description of the site as a garden implies great beauty and abundant provision. Hebrew narrative is normally quite spare in physical description,[17] but here the writer waxes eloquent about the richness of the first human domain. Rivers, precious metals, animals, "beautiful trees that produced delicious fruit"—all were found in the Garden. It was a wonderful place to live.

However, above all else, the Garden was a place of perfect harmony. God created Adam first, but then noted his loneliness and created Eve. Their union is described in terms that imply total relational fulfilment: "the two [were] united into one" (Gen. 2:24). Further, their union was undergirded by relationship with the Creator. God walked in the Garden with his creatures (Gen. 3:8). He spoke to them. The man and the woman could meet freely with God anywhere in the Garden. Genesis 2 gives us a picture of relational bliss.

Figure 3
The Loci of God's Special Presence

The Fall	Exodus	Completion of the Conquest of the Promised Land	First Coming of Christ	Second Coming of Christ
			Christ and the Church	New
Eden	Altars	Tabernacle	Temple	as the Temple	Jerusalem

AFTER THE FALL

Among the many trees that God created for the man and the woman, two stand out: the tree of life and the tree of the knowledge of good and evil. Nothing further is said in regard to the tree of life, so we may assume that Adam and Eve ate the fruit of that tree while they were in the Garden.[18] However, God specifically told them not to eat from the other tree. No reason is given for this restriction, and that in itself may have been part of the test. Would this blessed couple obey the one restriction given them by their Creator?

A new character now comes on the scene, the serpent, identified later in the Bible with Satan (Rev. 12:9; 20:2). This creature seduces the woman, who in turn seduces the man to eat the fruit of the tree and in essence rebel against their Maker. This episode, commonly called the fall, has many implications, but we will focus on the issues of relationship and the presence of God.

In brief, the fall resulted in alienation between Adam and Eve, to be sure, but even more fundamentally between God and the human couple. Ultimately, God removed them from the Garden, thus cutting them off from the tree of life. For the first time, death entered the world. God set powerful angelic creatures at the entrance to the Garden so Adam and Eve could not return. Driven from the Garden, Adam and Eve no longer had free, intimate, and easy access to the Creator. God was no longer present with them.

A knotty question arises at this point. The Bible clearly teaches that God is everywhere. In an essential sense, he is not absent from any portion of his creation. Theologians call this the doctrine of God's omnipresence. It is typified in the second stanza of Psalm 139:

> I can never escape from your spirit!
>   I can never get away from your presence!
> If I go up to heaven, you are there;
>   if I go down to the place of the dead, you are there.
> If I ride the wings of the morning,
>   if I dwell by the farthest oceans,
> even there your hand will guide me,
>   and your strength will support me.
> I could ask the darkness to hide me
>   and the light around me to become night—
>   but even in darkness I cannot hide from you.
> To you the night shines as bright as day.
>   Darkness and light are both alike to you. [Ps. 139:7–12]

Now in view of this biblical teaching, how can we speak of the absence of God?

Quite simply, on one level, God is present everywhere; nothing is beyond his ken. On another level, he is said to be present in some locales and absent from others. In this case theologians refer to God's special presence. That is to say, he makes his presence powerfully felt in certain locations but not in others. Given the fundamental alienation between God and humanity after the fall, it is appropriate to speak of God's special presence and his absence.

The (Pre-)Patriarchal Period

In the Garden there was no special place for divine-human encounter. There was no sanctuary, no holy place, because the entire Garden was holy. After the fall, however, a sanctuary was needed if human creatures were to meet their holy Creator. God would not meet them just anywhere in the creation; a special place had to be set aside. This arrangement symbolically signaled the gulf in the relationship between God and humanity. Sin separated them, and this fact had to be acknowledged.

It is in the context of the flood that we find the first mention of an altar.[19] After the flood waters receded, Noah and his family disembarked the ark. Then "Noah built an altar to the LORD and sacrificed on it the animals and birds that had been approved for that purpose" (Gen. 8:20). Although we do not get details, we can safely assume from later descriptions (e.g., Exod. 20:24–26) that it was a simple altar made out of earth or stones. Early altars were temporary structures, built out in the open.

As we enter the patriarchal period, we continue to read about the construction of altars and sacrifice, most often in the Abraham narrative.[20] Indeed, the narrative gives us the impression that Abraham constructed altars wherever he stopped for any length of time. His first recorded stop in the land of Canaan was Shechem, where it is said that the Lord appeared to him with a message reaffirming the promises of land and descendants, and Abraham responded by building "an altar there to commemorate the LORD's visit" (Gen. 12:7). In this case, Abraham constructed the altar in response to a theophany or appearance of God. Such an appearance marked the place as holy, so sacrifices had to be offered.

The narrative does not, however, link every instance of altar building with theophany. Indeed, in the very next verse (12:8), we learn that Abraham moved to a camp between Bethel and Ai and built an altar there so he could worship God. Thus altar building could be initiated either by God or by Abraham. The motivation in each case was to provide a place for fellowship between God and sinful human beings.

It is of great interest to note that when Abraham built an altar at Shechem and later at Hebron (Gen. 13:18), he placed them next to prominent trees. He built the former by the "oak at Moreh" (Gen. 12:6) and the latter near the "oak grove owned by Mamre" (Gen. 13:18). This association of sanctuary and trees was no fluke, for the original sanctuary was a garden filled with trees. We here have the first hints that these sacred places were reminiscent of the Garden.[21]

The altar built in Genesis 22 is extremely pertinent to later developments. In this passage, which is known in Jewish tradition as the *Akedah*, the "binding" of Isaac, Abraham is told to go to Mount Moriah in order to sacrifice his son. He goes there and builds the altar (22:9). Once Abraham has shown his unswerving trust, the Lord provides a substitute for the sacrifice. For our purposes, the location is crucial, but its significance is often missed. The mountain to which God commanded Abraham to go was Moriah (22:2). We read this name only one other time in the Bible, 2 Chronicles 3:1: "So Solomon began to build the Temple of the LORD in Jerusalem on Mount Moriah." Moriah thus appears to be another name for Zion.[22]

While the biblical narrative associates Abraham in particular with altar constructions, it is notable that both his son Isaac (Beer-sheba [Gen. 26:25]) and grandson Jacob (Shechem [Gen. 33:20]; Bethel [35:1, 3, 7]) are also associated with altar building. Even though the narrative is not concerned to tell us about all the activities of the patriarchs, including their altar constructions, we can detect a motivation beyond the obvious one of providing a place for the patriarchs and their families to fellowship with God in the new land. Remember that at this period in the history of God's people they have the promise of the land, but they don't yet possess it. By building altars through the land, they are in effect laying claim to it in God's name. By the end of the patriarchal period, altars that symbolize God's fellowship with his people dot the landscape of Canaan, anticipating events to come.

The Tabernacle

Between the end of the Book of Genesis and the beginning of Exodus some centuries have passed. The family of God, when they were received in Egypt, numbered only seventy (Gen. 46:27). By the time of the exodus this family had become a numerous people. The covenant at Sinai made formal the transition of God's people from a family to a nation (Exod. 19–24). A single open altar like that used by the patriarchs would no longer suffice for so numerous a people. If the people of God were to have any sense of corporate worship, then some kind of change had to take place. It was, of course, not up to the Israelites themselves to initiate such a change; God himself revealed his intention to Moses on Mount Sinai. He commanded Moses to build a tabernacle in which he could make his presence known in a special way (Exod. 25:9; 26:30).

At this time the Israelites were not a sedentary people. They were on the move. Inasmuch as the tabernacle was to serve as the central place of worship from the time the Israelites left Sinai until they were completely settled in the land, God would dwell in a mobile sanctuary. Like his people he would live in a tent-like structure.

At this point we can see that size was a factor in God's determination of the form for his place of worship. During the patriarchal period there had been only a few people, and the head of the clan could easily serve as a priestly type of mediator. Now that the people of God were numerous, he established a larger corporate place of worship. He also chose this time to institute the priesthood. No longer could the head of the clan handle the responsibilities required. A whole tribe (the Levites) was set apart for the task.

The focal point of the tabernacle was the Most Holy Place, where the ark, the most potent symbol of God's presence, was positioned. The Most Holy Place was set apart from the Holy Place by a curtain (Exod. 26:33). It was here that God was understood to be enthroned. The interior of the tabernacle was also filled with a cloud which represented his glory (Exod. 40:34–38; Num. 9:15–23). God was clearly present in the tabernacle.

The description of the tabernacle and its furniture is quite extensive in the Book of Exodus. Indeed, much of the second part is devoted to instructions for (chs. 25–31) and the actual building of the tabernacle (chs. 35–40). The strategically positioned interruption in chapters 32–34, the golden-calf incident, recounts the suppression of a rebellion against proper worship.[23] While we do not have the space to give a detailed explanation of the theological significance of the tabernacle and its accoutrements, we will provide a general outline as a counterbalance to the all-too-common arbitrary allegorical readings of the text.[24]

The tabernacle was a tent constructed of various metals, woods, and fabrics. Since the focal point was the Most Holy Place, it is no surprise to discover that as one moved in toward the center, more-expensive materials were used, reflecting an increasing intensity of holiness. Thus bronze was used for the bases of the poles which held up the linen separating the courtyard from the camp. But in moving from the periphery of the tabernacle toward the center there was a rough progression from bronze to silver to gold, until finally in the Most Holy Place was found "pure gold."

A similar progression can be seen in the fabrics. The fabric used to separate the courtyard from the camp was plain, though expensive, white linen. There was only one exception. At the entrance was a blue, purple, and scarlet linen, which surely was intended to attract attention to the entrance of the complex. For the tabernacle itself there are the innermost layer and three covers of different materials. The exact nature of the outermost fabric is debated; the Hebrew term *taḥaš* (Exod. 26:14; 36:19) is uncertain. The New International Version takes it as sea cow's hide; others suggest dolphin skin or "goatskin leather." All of these translations point to a material which is utilitarian. It is, after all, the outermost layer and has to withstand the elements. The second layer from the outside is made of "tanned ram skins." This, too, serves as protection, as does the next layer, which consists of "goat hair" (Exod. 26:7–13).

Special attention is given to the innermost layer. For it is the closest to the divine presence and is also the layer which would be seen, though but dimly (because lighting would be provided by only the menorah) and rarely (because few actually entered the tabernacle). Symbolically, the innermost layer gets at the heart of what the tabernacle is: "heaven on earth." Accordingly, the fabric is the most elaborate of all: "ten sheets of fine linen . . . are to be decorated with blue, purple, and scarlet yarn, with figures of cherubim skillfully embroidered into them" (Exod. 26:1). The expense of this fabric is indicated by the colors, which were extremely difficult to produce in antiquity and thus were usually reserved for royal garments. Note also that the innermost layer is a mixture of linen and wool. This is particularly striking in the light of Leviticus 19:19, which prohibits wearing clothing woven from two different kinds of fabric. Clearly such a mixture is reserved for holy purposes.

Imagine standing in the tabernacle and looking up toward the ceiling. The surface would be bluish—heaven-like—and populated with heavenly creatures, the powerful cherubim. In a word, one would be standing in heaven, or at least a symbolical heaven on earth. The tabernacle, the place God chose for his presence to dwell in a special way, was where heaven came into contact with earth.

Given its unique nature, the tabernacle was surrounded by all kinds of cultic protection. For instance, only certain classes of people could progress toward the Holy of Holies, and only after they offered the requisite sacrifices to atone for their sins. In addition, when the people of God encamped during the wilderness wanderings, the tabernacle was placed in the center of all the tribes. The Levites, the tribe set apart for priestly service, surrounded the tabernacle, creating a buffer against any who might intentionally or unintentionally profane the holy space. But the Levites could go only so far into the tabernacle area. Aaron's priestly descendants could go farther, but even they could not go into the Most Holy Place. This privilege was reserved for the high priest, and he could enter only on the Day of Atonement (Lev. 16).

A complete description of the tabernacle would include a section on the various objects that were placed inside. We have already mentioned the ark, and space permits brief mention of only one other, the lampstand. It was made out of gold, as befitted an object toward the center of the sacred space. What was particularly striking in its design was its treelike traits: "The entire lampstand and its decorations will be one piece—the base, center stem, lamp cups, buds, and blossoms. It will have six branches, three branches going out from each side of the center stem. Each of the six branches will hold a cup shaped like an almond blossom, complete with buds and petals" (Exod. 25:31–33). From this description it is clear that we are to understand the lampstand (menorah) as an almond tree.[25] Having already noted the association of the patriarchal altars with trees, we do not go too far to suggest again that the tree motif evokes memories of Eden.

The tabernacle continued in use for many years after the people of God entered the Promised Land. Unfortunately, we cannot provide a detailed history of its locations and use. The clearest picture comes from the early period of Samuel's life, when

Eli was judge, and the ark and tabernacle were located in Shiloh (1 Sam. 1–4).

The Temple

The next major transition in the story of God's making his presence known among his people comes with David and Solomon. It is at this time that the temple is built. In order to understand the transition, we must ask what the difference is between tabernacle and temple, and why the latter structure became appropriate at this point in the history of redemption.

At heart, the temple is very similar to the tabernacle. It is a structure that becomes increasingly holy toward the interior, culminating in the Holy of Holies at the back, where God is said to have made his presence known in a special way. The difference between temple and tabernacle is the difference between a house and a tent. A tent is a residence that can be packed up and moved. A house is a permanent structure. Thus the temple symbolizes permanence, establishment, firmness, a general trait confirmed by its innovative architectural features.

Special mention is made of the construction of two large pillars ("27 feet tall and 18 feet in circumference," 1 Kings 7:15). These pillars connote strength and permanence, grandeur and majesty, a fact brought out further by their names ("he [Huram] named the one on the south Jakin, and the one on the north Boaz," 1 Kings 7:21). Jakin likely should be translated "he establishes," while Boaz means "in him is strength."

Outside the temple proper was a large tank of water called the sea. It was the place where the priests would ritually wash in connection with their duties. The peculiar name by which this vessel was designated is of particular interest to us. Throughout the Near East the sea was a symbol of the forces of chaos, cosmic and historical.[26] In the Old Testament, Yahweh the creator God demonstrated his power by subduing the sea. We see this in the biblical poets (Job 12:15; Ps. 18:15) and the prophets

(Isa. 19:5; 27:1; Jer. 5:22; Dan. 7; Nah. 1:4). A large amount of water in a tank called the sea would certainly remind the people that God had conquered the forces of chaos and thus established a sense of permanence.

As an architectural structure symbolizing establishment and permanence, it is no coincidence that the temple came into existence shortly after the conquest was completed. This story actually begins in Deuteronomy 12, where Moses conveys to Israel in the wilderness God's instruction that they were to worship at one (and only one) permanent site. This regulation looked to the future, when they would be finally settled in the land. Indeed, it would go into effect only "when you drive out the nations that live there" (Deut. 12:2). Accordingly, the first proposal to build a temple comes in a chapter that begins, "The LORD had brought peace to the land" (2 Sam. 7:1). God, through David, had driven out the Philistines and brought the Israelites to a new level of security.

When the time seems right to build the temple, David has a dialogue with the prophet Nathan. The discussion revolves around the Hebrew word *bayit* (alternatively translated throughout the chapter as "house," "temple," "palace," and "dynasty").[27] David begins by lamenting the disparity of his living in a beautiful palace *(bayit)* while the ark is housed in a tent (and probably an aged one at that). Nathan initially responds by affirming David's intentions, but that night the Lord appears to him with the message that David is not the one to build his "temple" *(bayit)*.

God's reasons for not allowing David to build the temple are instructive. First, God inquires, "Are you the one to build me a temple to live in?" In other words, it is God who initiates the building of his residence; no human person has that right. A quick look back at the tabernacle narratives reminds us that it was God who initiated its building as well as delivered to Moses the architectural plans (see, e.g., Exod. 26:30). Second, as David recalls when giving instructions before his death, the Lord had said to him earlier, "You must not build a temple to honor my name, for you are a warrior and have shed much blood" (1 Chron. 28:3). Many readers of the Bible misunderstand this to mean that God would not allow a person who had been engaged in killing to perform such a holy task as building his temple. This, however, does not take into account the fact that it was God himself who instructed and guided David in the waging of holy war. No, God's words have a redemptive-historical rather than ethical significance. David had the role of completing the conquest, and since the temple symbolized peace from enemies, the task was better left to his successor, whose very name—Solomon—meant "peace."

It is not within our present purpose to develop further the theology of 2 Samuel 7, also known as the Davidic covenant, but we would be remiss not to broadly outline God's response to David. David, because he dwelt in a beautiful *bayit* ("palace"), had offered to build God a *bayit* ("temple"). God declined the offer, but then conferred on David the gift of a *bayit* ("dynasty," 2 Sam. 7:11).

In accordance with God's will, David did not build the temple, but the Book of 1 Chronicles indicates that he exerted great effort preparing for its construction.[28] The temple was built and dedicated by Solomon with words that indicated a clear understanding that, while God made his presence known in the temple, he did not really live there: "But will God really live on earth? Why, even the highest heavens cannot contain you. How much less this Temple I have built!" (1 Kings 8:27).

Centuries later the people of Israel made the fatal mistake of treating the temple as God's permanent residence. They did not trust God; rather, they regarded the temple as a kind of idol that assured them of God's presence and protection. This is the heart of Jeremiah's temple sermon (ch. 7) accusing the people of not responding to God's call for repentance. Instead, they presumed on his protection since he lived in Jerusalem. As long as the temple was there, God would never allow their city to be harmed, would he?

Ezekiel 9 through 11 narrates God's response to this question. These chapters show God rising from his throne in the Holy of Holies, moving to the entrance (9:3), mounting his cherubim-driven chariot, and heading east toward Babylon (11:23). The next time he is seen he is at the head of the Babylonian army, which destroys Jerusalem and tears down the temple. It is true that after purification a remnant ultimately returns to the land. This remnant then builds a second temple, where God once again makes his presence known among the people. But compared to the previous temple, it "must seem like nothing at all" (Hag. 2:3). A greater glory is yet to come.

Christ as the Temple

On the surface the Old Testament and the New seem quite different in regard to the presence of God. In the Old Testament God seems distant; he is approached only with fear, trembling, and sacrifice. He is present only in certain geographical locales, and these places, whether altar, tabernacle, or temple, are surrounded with prohibitions and taboos. In the New Testament, however, God seems close to us. We can have an intimate relationship with him. We may call him "Abba," Aramaic for "daddy" (Rom. 8:15). It seems quite a contrast, and it is, as Hebrews 12 indicates. After all, we today have not come to a physical mountain like Sinai, a fearful place that we don't want to approach (vv. 18–21); rather, we have come to "Mount Zion, to the city of the living God, the heavenly Jerusalem, and to thousands of angels in joyful assembly" (v. 22). However, reading the New Testament carefully shows that this is not a true contrast. For the Old Testament is actually the foundation for our intimate relationship with God in the New. In a word, Jesus Christ is the new tabernacle, the new temple of God.

Remember that the issue is God's presence among us. The New Testament teaches, of course, that Jesus is God himself. The prologue of John tells us that the Word became flesh and "lived here on earth among us" (1:14). Most English translations do not catch the force of the Greek. The word "lived" translates *skēnoō*, which is the verbal form of "tabernacle" *(skēnē)*. Jesus came and "tabernacled among us." John is indicating the arrival of someone who will replace the architectural places of worship.

In John 4, another passage that relates to the issue at hand, Jesus talks to a Samaritan woman. The Samaritans and the Jews had a running controversy as to the proper place to worship the Lord. The latter felt that God had chosen Mount Zion, but the former worshiped God on Mount Gerizim near the city of Shechem. Jesus addresses this theological problem by suggesting that someone has come who will make this question obsolete: "The time is coming and is already here when true worshipers will worship the Father in spirit and in truth. The Father is looking for anyone who will worship him that way. For God is Spirit, so those who worship him must worship in spirit and truth" (John 4:23–24). While in this context Jesus affirms the earlier practice of the Jews who worshiped at Zion, his comment implies that the temple is no longer needed.

That the temple is no longer needed becomes explicit in Mark 13, where Jesus comments on the future. While walking with Jesus in the temple precincts (as restored by Herod the Great), the disciples are amazed by the sight and exclaim, "Teacher, look at these tremendous buildings! Look at the massive stones in the walls!" Jesus shocks them by responding, "These magnificent buildings will be so completely demolished that not one stone will be left on top of another" (Mark 13:2). This statement becomes an occasion for his talk about the future, the so-called little apocalypse. Later, during his trial before the high priest, he is accused of saying that he would destroy the temple and in three days raise it again (Mark 14:55–59). While the testimony is likely distorted, it is certainly provocative. At any rate, the Gospel writers clearly understood Jesus to be putting himself in the place of the temple. While the temple was the site where God made his presence known, Jesus himself is the presence of God among humankind. He is the reality to which the temple looked forward.

The metaphor of Christ as the temple is used flexibly in the rest of the New Testament. In the Epistles, for instance, Christians are compared to the temple, either individually (1 Cor. 6:19) or corporately (1 Cor. 3:16–17). For just as God was present in the Holy of Holies, so the Holy Spirit dwells in the Christian. Significantly, however, Peter refers to the church as the temple, but notes that it is Christ who is "the living cornerstone of God's temple" (1 Peter 2:4).

The idea that Christ is the fulfilment of the temple fits the New Testament's understanding of the relationship between Christ and the entire worship apparatus of the Old Testament. This point is particularly developed by the Book of Hebrews, which teaches that Christ is the fulfilment of sacrifice and the priesthood. Jesus Christ is the perfect sacrifice and perfect priest (Heb. 9:11–10:18).

To complete the theme of the presence of God in the Bible, we must press on to the Book of Revelation. In the final two chapters of that book, we get a glimpse of the world to come, the new heaven and new earth. Strikingly, we read that "no temple could be seen in the city, for the Lord God Almighty and the Lamb are its temple" (21:22). No longer is there the need for a special holy place. Sin has been eradicated, and God and humanity again live in harmony and bliss. Not surprisingly, we find allusions to the Garden at the end of the canon: "And the angel showed me a pure river with the water of life, clear as crystal, flowing from the throne of God and of the Lamb, coursing down the center of the main street. On each side of the river grew a tree of life, bearing twelve crops of fruit, with a fresh crop each month. The leaves were used for medicine to heal the nations" (22:1–2). This is the climax of redemptive history. The restoration of Eden, but more than restoration. The imagery, including the two trees of life, suggests that our heavenly Eden will surpass the original.

We began this chapter by posing the question, "Is the God of the Old Testament the same as the God of the New Testament?" We were driven to ask this question because a superficial reading of the Bible might lead a person to contrast the pictures of deity presented in the two Testaments. Is the God of the Old Testament distant, cold, angry, judgmental, arbitrary? Is the God of the New Testament, particularly as we see him in his Son, Jesus Christ, warm, intimate, personal, gracious, and caring?

We observed that the Bible avoids speculation and abstractions about God; instead, it paints word pictures of the relationship between God and his people. We chose to examine three of these themes to see whether or not the God of the Old Testament is different from the God of the New. In our exploration we saw how the covenants of the Old Testament drove forward to the new covenant. We marveled as Yahweh the warrior of the Old Testament anticipated the battles of Jesus in the New Testament. We followed the story of how God's dwelling with his people overcame humanity's rebellion to lead from the Garden to the New Jerusalem.

Our study has led to the conclusion that the Bible presents a unified picture of God. The God of the New Testament is clearly the God of the Old Testament. This unified picture, however, is not a static one. God progressively reveals himself to his people through time. The shadows of the Old Testament give way to the reality of the New. Looking to Jesus Christ as the fulfilment of the Old Testament, Augustine summarized it well: "The New Testament is in the Old concealed; the Old Testament is in the New revealed."

How Is the Christian to Apply the Old Testament to Life?

In chapter 2 we explored why Christians see discontinuity between the God of the Old and the God of the New Testament. While concluding that the two are one, we saw that biblical revelation progressed through time. God revealed more and more of himself until Jesus Christ, God himself, dwelt among us. We saw how the whole Old Testament anticipated the coming of Christ. He fulfilled the expectation found there. Thus the relationship between the Old and New Testaments is one of continuity and discontinuity. There is continuity because the God of the Old and New Testaments is the same God. There is continuity because Jesus Christ is anticipated in the Old Testament and revealed in the New. However, discontinuity results from the greater clarity which is associated with the revelation of God's Son:

> Long ago God spoke many times and in many ways to our ancestors through the prophets. But now in these final days, he has

spoken to us through his Son. God promised everything to the Son as an inheritance, and through the Son he made the universe and everything in it. The Son reflects God's own glory, and everything about him represents God exactly. He sustains the universe by the mighty power of his command. After he died to cleanse us from the stain of sin, he sat down in the place of honor at the right hand of the majestic God of heaven. [Heb. 1:1–3]

With this background we turn now to the question of how the Old Testament continues to direct Christians in their obedience to God. It is easy to become confused about this question when we look at isolated passages in the New Testament. Consider what Jesus said about the law when he delivered the Sermon on the Mount:

> Don't misunderstand why I have come. I did not come to abolish the law of Moses or the writings of the prophets. No, I came to fulfill them. I assure you, until heaven and earth disappear, even the smallest detail of God's law will remain until its purpose is achieved. So if you break the smallest commandment and teach others to do the same, you will be the least in the Kingdom of Heaven. But anyone who obeys God's laws and teaches them will be great in the Kingdom of Heaven.
>
> But I warn you—unless you obey God better than the teachers of religious law and the Pharisees do, you can't enter the Kingdom of Heaven at all! [Matt. 5:17–20]

Is the Christian then bound to the "jot and tittle" of the law?[1] If so, what are we to make of Paul's words:

> So then, dear friends, the point is this: The law no longer holds you in its power, because you died to its power when you died with Christ on the cross. And now you are united with the one who was raised from the dead. As a result, you can produce good fruit, that is, good deeds for God. When we were con-

trolled by our old nature, sinful desires were at work within us, and the law aroused these evil desires that produced sinful deeds, resulting in death. But now we have been released from the law, for we died with Christ, and we are no longer captive to its power. Now we can really serve God, not in the old way by obeying the letter of the law, but in the new way, by the Spirit. [Rom. 7:4–6]

So do we obey the law of the Old Testament?

Different Viewpoints

We will cite two different schools of thought as contemporary representatives of the poles of opinion on this matter,[2] though there are a variety of viewpoints within these two approaches.[3] At heart dispensationalism and theonomy are hermeneutical stances, but they both focus on the law in specific ways. One finds a tendency in dispensationalist writing to distinguish between the Old Testament as a time when God worked through law and the New Testament as a period of grace. To quote C. I. Scofield: "The most obvious and striking division of the word of truth is that between Law and Grace. Indeed, these contrasting principles *characterize* the two most important dispensations—Jewish and Christian. . . . Scripture never, in *any* dispensation, mingles these two principles."[4] This view, which many contemporary dispensationalists do not hold to so explicitly, cannot help but lead to a minimalization of the law, a disregard for the Old Testament law as such. It does not, as Bruce Waltke points out, take into account Paul's assertion that the law is "holy and right and good" (Rom. 7:12).[5]

On the other hand, the school of thought that goes by the name theonomy (Greek for "law of God") or Christian reconstruction argues that the Old Testament laws and penalties are still in effect today.[6] The influence of this school was at its height during the late 1970s and early 1980s. Fortunately, this influence is dissipating, but there is some hangover effect on the religious right.

In brief, theonomy's approach to the law is to take Jesus' words seriously, dogmatically, and literally. The "jot and tittle" of the law is still in effect. Strict continuity is assumed between the Old and New Testaments.[7] Theonomists believe that it is the job of government to enforce Old Testament law, which thereby becomes a blueprint for contemporary society.

In the light of passages like Hebrews 7–10, theonomists acknowledge that the laws relating to the formal worship apparatus of Israel no longer apply. Jesus was the perfect sacrifice, served as the ideal high priest, and manifested the presence of God, thus replacing the temple. However, the moral law and the civil law, along with their accompanying penalties, maintain their force. In other words, theonomy does not recognize any distinction between the Ten Commandments and those Old Testament laws that concerned specific situations (i.e., case laws).

Theonomy and dispensationalism represent two extreme approaches to the law. While rigorously orthodox in their theology, they radically disagree on the relationship between the Old and New Testaments. The former stresses the continuity between the Old and New Testaments, while the latter emphasizes the discontinuity. Through Bible schools, seminaries, and widely used Bible-study helps, dispensationalism has had a huge impact on the twentieth-century American church.[8] Theonomy's appeal increased in the late 1970s and early 1980s as Christians grew frustrated with a culture that they found hostile to their faith. As Christians became increasingly political, many wanted to ground their legal and political thinking in the Bible, and it seemed a matter of common sense that the Bible's own laws be the basis of this system.

However, there are weaknesses in theonomy. We need to point out first that the Old Testament law addressed the people of God when they were a nation. God's people were a distinct political entity, the nation of Israel; and a major function of the so-called case laws and particularly their penalties was to keep this chosen

nation free from sin. Today God does not work through a chosen nation, but through a chosen people comprising the nations
of the world. This element of discontinuity has major impact on
how we should observe the law. Second, God gave Israel the law
at a time before Jesus Christ was revealed to the world. We have
already suggested that this has a clear impact on the observance
of the ceremonial law; we shall soon see that it also affects much
of the rest of the law.

In short, upon reflection we cannot assume simple continuity between the Testaments in the matter of the observance of
the law and its penalties. Key passages in the New Testament
confirm that something new is at work. At this point we will look
at only one law, that concerning adultery. Adultery is condemned
by the seventh commandment (Exod. 20:14; Deut. 5:18). The
case law informs us of the penalty: "If a man is discovered com-
mitting adultery, both he and the other man's wife must be killed.
In this way, the evil will be cleansed from Israel" (Deut. 22:22;
see also Lev. 20:10). On the basis of this Old Testament regulation, theonomy argues that adultery today deserves the death
penalty. Attentive reading of the New Testament, however, indicates otherwise. We think first of John 7:53–8:11, the account
of the woman caught in adultery. It is true that this episode is
not found in the earliest manuscripts, yet many scholars take it
as authentic material concerning Jesus' life. The woman was an
adulteress. She was about to be stoned, but Jesus intervened and
halted the proceeding with the challenge "Let those who have
never sinned throw the first stones!" (8:7). Turning to the
woman, he told her that he did not condemn her. He then sent
her away with the warning to "sin no more" (v. 11).

If we are unwilling to decide the issue on the basis of a suspect
text, we may appeal to Jesus' teaching on divorce. In essence,
Jesus substitutes divorce for the death penalty. If a spouse is caught
in the act of adultery, divorce is permitted instead of the death
penalty (Matt. 5:31–32). In this regard we should also point out

that Jesus intensified our understanding of the law of adultery. In Jesus' eyes adultery is not simply the act of illicit intercourse, it is the lustful look. Thus we would all be subject to the penalty of the law (Matt. 5:27–30).

It is clear that neither dispensationalism nor theonomy provides an adequate basis for understanding the law of the Old Testament. The former does not allow for the element of continuity that we observe in the New Testament; and the latter, in its simple assertion of strict continuity, does not take account of the discontinuity between the Testaments. To gain a proper understanding of the Christian's responsibility as regards the law, we must closely examine the law of the Old Testament for clues into the New Testament's guidance on this matter.

The Nature of Old Testament Law

The law is the collection of requirements God imposed on Israel during the time of Moses. More than six hundred such requirements guided Israel's obedience to God. We find them collected in three main places in the Pentateuch (the first five books of the Old Testament). The oldest collection is likely the so-called book of the covenant (Exod. 20:1–23:33, named in 24:7). The latest is found in the laws of Deuteronomy (4:44–29:1; "Deuteronomy" is Greek for "second law"). This law is given by Moses on the plains of Moab just before his death and the Israelites' entry into the Promised Land. Moses' purpose is to warn the Israelites not to sin as they sinned in the wilderness. Accordingly, he repeats (often with variation) elements given in the earlier law codes. Significantly, both the book of the covenant and the Deuteronomic law code begin with the Ten Commandments (Exod. 20:1–17 and Deut. 5:6–21).

Leviticus and Numbers are sandwiched between the two great law codes. Like Exodus and Deuteronomy, they are books which interweave narrative and law. The legal prescriptions found in

Leviticus and Numbers focus primarily on the formal worship of Israel, that is, on regulations concerning the priesthood, sacrifices, and ritual purity. The laws in Leviticus 1–7, for example, either inform or remind the priests how to perform certain sacrificial ceremonies.

Some of the laws in Leviticus that determined whether a person was clean or unclean are hard for us to relate to today. For us, the matter of cleanness and uncleanness has to do with physical hygiene. For the ancient priests, it had to do with religious purity. To be clean meant to be in the right state to approach the powerful and holy God. To approach God in a state of uncleanness would mean certain doom.

Uncleanness was contagious in the sense that coming into contact with certain objects or people meant catching their uncleanness. Such objects were not necessarily sinful. To the contrary, they may have been excessively holy and thus protected by taboos. Blood and semen, fluids that were crucial, respectively, to sacrifice and to fulfilment of the promise of descendants, were treated with special respect (Lev. 15; 17:10–12). Coming into contact with them rendered a person unclean because they were so critical, not because they were dirty or sinful.

A similar consideration determined which foods were kosher (i.e., clean). Certain meats were prohibited, but not because they were considered unhealthy. It's more likely that they were viewed as not representative of the pure species of creation. The clean animals had certain characteristics that the unclean animals lacked. For instance, land animals that might be eaten had to chew the cud and have a split hoof (Lev. 11:1–8). Camels, rabbits, and pigs didn't qualify. This division of clean and unclean animals had a counterpart among humanity, which was similarly divided into clean (Israelite) and unclean (Gentile). When the latter distinction was abolished because of the work of Christ, so was the former distinction.

Moral, Civil, and Ceremonial Law

As we survey the laws of Moses, we note that they deal with a wide variety of important issues that concern the relationship between God and humanity as well as between human beings. For instance, while we have seen that the bulk of laws in the books of Leviticus and Numbers concern the formal worship of Israel, there are also laws that concern the Israelite as a citizen as well as specific moral prescriptions. Exodus and Deuteronomy likewise contain laws that concern humans as moral beings, citizens, and worshipers.

Accordingly, it is common practice today to distinguish three types of Old Testament laws. Besides moral law, there are also civil and ceremonial law. It is also commonly pointed out today that the Israelites themselves apparently did not make this distinction, since the three types of law are interwoven in the codes. They are not distinguished. The Israelites did not think in terms of religious and secular spheres. All of life was religious to them. In spite of the fact that this threefold division was not native to Israel, we will find it useful as we grapple with our own responsibility toward the law of the Old Testament.

First, moral law states God's principles for a right relationship with him and with others. The Ten Commandments are the most visible and powerful expression of God's will for his people. As we read the New Testament and reflect on the Bible as a whole, we see that these commands are still operative. Thus Jesus heartily approved a legal expert's summary of the Ten Commandments: "'You must love the Lord your God with all your heart, all your soul, all your strength, and all your mind.' And, 'Love your neighbor as yourself'" (Luke 10:27).

Second are the civil laws. These laws regulated Israel as the nation chosen by God to be his special people. For instance, Deuteronomy 17:14–20 tells the people how they should choose a king. Inasmuch as the king will have the same powers and authority as do the kings of the nations around Israel (v. 14), the office of king isn't defined. However, his power is limited, since he is to be a reflection of a far greater King—God. No king of Israel, therefore, is to abuse his power by taking many wives or amassing personal wealth. On the positive side, as a leader of the people he is to be an avid student of God's Word. As the nation chosen to reflect God's power and love to all other nations, such laws are crucial for Israel.

The third division, ceremonial law, defines how Israel was to worship God. Examples include the laws commanding and describing the ritual for the sacrifice of a whole burnt offering (Lev. 1). Other ceremonial laws include regulations regarding the priesthood and the place of worship as well as the festivals that celebrated Yahweh's great acts in history.

The Ten Commandments and the Case Law

Before we can determine how we today are to obey Old Testament law, we must make one other distinction, one that was not only known by but fundamental to the Old Testament people of God. At the base of the law of the Old Testament are the Ten Commandments. Even in an age of rapidly decreasing biblical literacy, most people have heard of the Ten Commandments. Perhaps Cecil B. DeMille is more responsible for this than are today's preachers.[9] Tragically, recent statistics indicate that while people today have heard of the Ten Commandments, they are unable to identify any of the specific commands. For that reason it seems appropriate to cite the text here:

I am the LORD your God, who rescued you from slavery in Egypt.

Do not worship any other gods besides me.

Do not make idols of any kind, whether in the shape of birds or animals or fish. You must never worship or bow down to them, for I, the LORD your God, am a jealous God who will not share your affection with any other god! I do not leave unpunished the sins of those who hate me, but I punish the children for the sins of their parents to the third and fourth generations. But I lavish my love on those who love me and obey my commands, even for a thousand generations.

Do not misuse the name of the LORD your God. The LORD will not let you go unpunished if you misuse his name.

Remember to observe the Sabbath day by keeping it holy. Six days a week are set apart for your daily duties and regular work, but the seventh day is a day of rest dedicated to the LORD your God. On that day no one in your household may do any kind of work. This includes you, your sons and daughters, your male and female servants, your livestock, and any foreigners living among you. For in six days the LORD made the heavens, the earth, the sea, and everything in them; then he rested on the seventh day. That is why the LORD blessed the Sabbath day and set it apart as holy.

Honor your father and mother. Then you will live a long, full life in the land the LORD your God will give you.

Do not murder.

Do not commit adultery.

Do not steal.

Do not testify falsely against your neighbor.

Do not covet your neighbor's house. Do not covet your neighbor's wife, male or female servant, ox or donkey, or anything else your neighbor owns. [Exod. 20:2–17]

So much can be and has been said about this short section of Scripture that we cannot hope even to scratch the surface of it here![10] Fortunately, our purpose does not include a detailed exposition of the laws. Rather, we seek to understand how God intends the Old Testament law to direct our lives today. To accomplish that purpose, we need first to highlight certain aspects of the nature and function of the Ten Commandments.

It is crucial theologically to note the literary and redemptive-historical contexts of the Ten Commandments. The two contexts are really intertwined here. We saw in chapter 2 that the law, and the Ten Commandments in particular, is part of the larger treaty form. It flows from history, in this case the history of God's grace toward Israel. It is not incidental, then, that the commandments are prefaced by a historical prologue that recalls the deliverance from Egypt. Thus it is clear that the law given to Israel at Sinai occurs in the context of a gracious relationship; it does not establish that relationship.

We would also point out that the Ten Commandments came on two tablets. The significance of this fact is unclear. It is possible that the two tablets are two copies of the commandments, reflecting ancient Near Eastern treaty-making practice. Another possibility, equally speculative, is that the two tablets divided the first four commandments, which concern divine-human relationships, from the other six, which focus on human-human relationships. This conceptual distinction occurs as well in Jesus' summary of the law: "'You must love the Lord your God with all your heart, all your soul, and all your mind.' This is the first and greatest commandment. A second is equally important: 'Love your neighbor as yourself'" (Matt. 22:37–38).

The Ten Commandments are highly unusual in their ancient Near Eastern context in that they express general ethical-theological principles. A technical term often used for this is apodictic law. Most ancient Near Eastern law (as well as most biblical law) is case law, that is, law that concerns specific situations.[11] Richard Averbeck describes the difference well: apodictic laws are "laws that unconditionally and categorically assert right and wrong"; case laws "define specific cases and prescribe legal consequences."[12]

With this general background, we turn our attention now to the relationship between the Ten Commandments and the case laws with their attendant penalties. As we move from the former to the latter, we see a clear transition from general ethical precepts to specific situations. Along with this transition we as Christians find ourselves further distanced from the text in that it is harder to see the relevance for our lives.

Between the Decalogue and the case laws in the Book of Exodus there is a short narrative describing the people's reaction to the appearance of God on Mount Sinai. Moses then went into "the deep darkness where God was" (Exod. 20:21), and here God spoke further: "And the LORD said to Moses, 'Say this to the people of Israel: You are witnesses that I have spoken to you from heaven. Remember, you must not make or worship idols of silver or gold. The altars you make for me must be simple altars of earth. Offer on such altars your sacrifices to me'" (Exod. 20:22–24; see also vv. 25–26). Thus after an echo of the first two commandments God gives the first case law, which informs the Israelites how they are to construct an altar. Our contemporary reaction to this law is quite different from our reaction to the Ten Commandments. What in the world does this case law have to do with us or our society today? We do not build altars, nor do we offer sacrifices.

A similar situation prevails in the next section, the law concerning the treatment of Hebrew slaves. The text begins, "If you buy a Hebrew slave, he is to serve for only six years. Set him free in the seventh year . . ." (Exod. 21:2a; see also vv. 2b–11). But we have no slaves, and in particular we have no Hebrew slaves. Again, the distance between us and the case law is manifest.

Let's now skip down to the goring-ox law:

> If a bull gores a man or woman to death, the bull must be stoned, and its flesh may not be eaten. In such a case, however, the owner will not be held liable. Suppose, on the other hand, that the owner knew the bull had gored people in the past, yet the bull was not kept under control. If this is true and if the bull kills someone, it must be stoned, and the owner must also be killed. However, the dead person's relatives may accept payment from the owner of the bull to compensate for the loss of life. The owner will have to pay whatever is demanded. [Exod. 21:28–30]

I used to live in urban Philadelphia. Very few people I knew there would be affected by such a law. Again, the point is that we feel distanced from the law.

Let's turn our attention to the Book of Deuteronomy, the second place where we find the Decalogue. Once again we find the Ten Commandments at the head of a long section of other laws (Deut. 5:6–21). And again we find that those laws that follow seem to be totally irrelevant to us today. Consider, for instance, Deuteronomy 22:8: "Every new house you build must have a barrier around the edge of its flat rooftop. That way you will not bring the guilt of bloodshed on your household if someone falls from the roof." Does our observance of the law of God require that we build a protective barrier around our roofs?

A further issue is the penalties associated with case law.[13] Theonomic thinkers like Greg Bahnsen believe that God intends the penology of the Old Testament case law to be operative today in modern nations. He notes that there is no provision for a prison system. While restitution is required in some cases, the preeminent penalty for breaking the law is death. Indeed, the Old Testament law calls for the death penalty in cases of "murder, adultery and unchastity, sodomy and bestiality, homosexuality, rape, incest, incorrigibility in children, sabbath breaking, kidnapping, apostasy, witchcraft, sorcery, and false pretension to prophecy, and blasphemy."[14] Rousas Rushdoony adds offering human sacrifice, sacrificing to false gods, propagating false doctrines, rejecting a decision of the court, and failing to restore bail.[15] Rushdoony argues that a consistent use of the death penalty would radically reduce crime by eliminating the criminal element from our society and also by providing a deterrent. In order to heighten the deterrent value of capital punishment, he would like to have public executions.[16] In addition, minors, the insane, and the mentally deficient should be treated like anyone else in the courtroom and thus be subject to the death penalty if convicted of a capital crime.[17]

In summary, we conclude that the case law of the Old Testament, as opposed to the Ten Commandments, is foreign to those of us who live in an industrial-urban setting at the beginning of the third millennium after Christ. In addition, the penalties strike us as harsh. What should our response be? Should we endeavor to conform our thinking and behavior to the biblical case-law as the theonomists urge us to do? Or should we maintain that the Old Testament law makes no difference because we are living in the period of grace? Actually, we will find that neither of these responses is adequate to our understanding of biblical revelation or to our contemporary needs.

From Specific to General

A closer look at the case law reveals that these specific laws are not laws in addition to the Ten Commandments. On the contrary, the specific laws flow from the general ethical principles asserted in the commandments. Let's illustrate with the law of the goring ox and the command to build a fence around the roof of a house.

The intent of the law concerning the goring ox is to protect life. If an ox gores a person, it must be destroyed. Not having known any better at the time, the owner is not morally culpable. However, if the ox is not destroyed and then kills a second person, the situation is totally different. Not only the ox, but also the owner is put to death. The owner, through negligence or willful rejection of the law, has caused the death of another human being. He is therefore guilty of murder, breaking the sixth commandment. He deserves the death penalty. Note that the goring-ox law is a specific outworking of the commandment.

What about the Deuteronomic law about building fences on the roof of a house? Why should anyone build such a fence? We must realize the function of a roof in ancient Palestine. People used the roof as if it were a room of the house. Its role was something like that of a porch today. Because houses in the hilly areas of Israel were built on inclines, the possibility of falling off a roof was real. So the case law served the purpose of protecting human life. Like the law of the goring ox, it was an outworking of the sixth commandment, "Do not murder."

These two examples illustrate the relationship between the Decalogue and the rest of the law. The latter flows from the former. A number of studies have demonstrated this on a grand scale, at least in regard to the Book of Deuteronomy. The most convenient study, and one with an evangelical view of Scripture, is that done by Walter Kaiser.[18] He argues that the entire law section of the Book of Deuteronomy flows from the fountainhead provided by the Ten Commandments. He begins by showing that Deuteronomy 5–11 is a commentary on the first commandment. The following chapters similarly serve as commentaries on specific commandments:

12:1–31: The First and Second Commandments
13:1–14:27: The Third Commandment
14:28–16:17: The Fourth Commandment
16:18–18:22: The Fifth Commandment
19:1–22:8: The Sixth Commandment
22:9–23:18: The Seventh Commandment
23:19–24:7: The Eighth Commandment
24:8–25:4: The Ninth Commandment
25:5–16: The Tenth Commandment

While the case laws in Exodus do not have the same sequential precision, it does not take a great deal of ingenuity to suggest connections with the Ten Commandments. We conclude that the case laws of the Old Testament are applications of the Ten Commandments to the specific situations of the Old Testament people of God.

At this point we must mention an important principle that runs through the Old and New Testaments. We are not saved by the law or by our obedience. For the ancient Israelites in slavery in Egypt and for modern American Christians, salvation comes only by the grace of God. As Paul forcefully stated, "No one can ever be made right in God's sight by doing what his law commands. For the more we know God's law, the clearer it becomes that we aren't obeying it" (Rom. 3:20). The role of the law remains the same today as in the past: it is our gracious God's guideline for living that pleases him and is good for us.

As Christians, we know in a special way our inability to keep the law. We know we are lawbreakers. Paul reaffirms the universal sinfulness of humanity by quoting a pastiche of Old Testament texts:

> "No one is good—
> not even one.
> No one has real understanding,
> no one is seeking God.
> All have turned away from God;
> all have gone wrong.
> No one does good,
> not even one."
> "Their talk is foul, like the stench from an open grave.
> Their speech is filled with lies."
> "The poison of a deadly snake drips from their lips."
> "Their mouths are full of cursing and bitterness."
> "They are quick to commit murder.
> Wherever they go, destruction and misery follow them.
> They do not know what true peace is."
> "They have no fear of God to restrain them." [Rom. 3:10–18]

And it is not a matter of quantity of sin. James reminds those of us who might try to get by on our relative goodness that "the person who keeps all of the laws except one is as guilty as the person who has broken all of God's laws. For the same God who said, 'Do not commit adultery,' also said, 'Do not murder.' So if you murder someone, you have broken the entire law, even if you do not commit adultery" (James 2:10–11).

But the human plight is even more desperate. In the light of the Sermon on the Mount (Matt. 5–7), where Jesus intensifies the law, it is hard to believe that there are many people who have not committed adultery. In his teaching, all the law takes on a radically internal understanding. Consider, for instance, his comments about the seventh commandment:

> You have heard that the law of Moses says, "Do not commit adultery." But I say, anyone who even looks at a woman with lust in his eye has already committed adultery with her in his heart. So if your eye—even if it is your good eye—causes you to lust, gouge it out and throw it away. It is better for you to lose one part of your body than for your whole body to be thrown into hell. And if your hand—even if it is your stronger hand—causes you to sin, cut it off and throw it away. It is better for you to lose one part of your body than for your whole body to be thrown into hell. [Matt. 5:27–30]

After reading a passage like this, it is good to remind ourselves that Jesus is our perfect high priest as well as our once-and-for-all sacrifice. In other words, Jesus took our sins on himself and offered himself as a sacrifice in our place (Heb. 5:1–10; 7:15–8:13; 10:1–18).

But how, then, does the Old Testament law affect us? Clearly Jesus and the apostles appealed to many of the provisions of the Decalogue. Idolatry, blasphemy, cursing one's parents, stealing, adultery, murder, lying, and coveting were still wrong. The general ethical principles of the Ten Commandments were still incumbent on the New Testament believer. But what about the case law?

As we investigate the continuity and discontinuity between the Old and New Testaments, we must recall that in its Old Testament setting the case law was best understood as the specification of the Ten Commandments. In particular, the case law was the applica-

tion of the Ten Commandments to the sociological and redemptive-historical context of the people of God at the time—the
nation of Israel. The Old Testament case law, then, is not directly
applicable to Christians today. For we differ in at least three fundamental ways from the ancient Israelites. First, they were primarily agriculturalists. Second, it was *as a nation* that the Israelites
were the people of God. Third, and most significantly, they lived
at an earlier point of redemptive history than we do. In a word,
they lived in the period before Christ's earthly ministry, and we
live in a period after Christ has come. Consider also that there is
no specific Old Testament case law concerned with, for example,
the selling of illicit drugs. We look in vain for such a law. Fur-
thermore, we look in vain for laws that specifically deal with abor-
tion, thievery via computers, and pornography, though most orthodox Christians consider such activities immoral or criminal. Of
what relevance, then, are the Old Testament case laws?

While the Old Testament case laws are not directly applicable
to us, they do illustrate ethical principles that are relevant today.
By studying how they worked in ancient Israel and asking what
in them pertains to today, we can discover their continued relevance. Let's again consider the case of the goring ox, which was
an outworking of the sixth commandment. Even in its Old Testament context it was a concretization of a general ethical principle that would need flexible application by the courts of Israel.
For instance, what if the offending animal was not an ox, but a
butting goat that killed a child? Surely the same principles applied
in that case. And today, even in our cities, we can see analogous
cases. We may not have goring oxen in urban areas, but we do
have people who keep pitbulls. A number of these dogs have seriously maimed and even killed. The case could be made that the
owner of such a dog (or any malicious dog) is responsible on the
second attack. In addition, a breed of dog that shows a propensity toward doing serious bodily harm could perhaps be prohibited by legislation.

Our second example, the law that requires a fence around a roof, likewise shows us that while Old Testament case law does not give us a blueprint for contemporary regulations, it does give us principles that we can ponder, debate, and ultimately apply to contemporary society. It is true, of course, that a literal application of this law to modern American society would be foolish, since we do not use our roofs as a room of the house. But we can immediately sense the relevance of this law today by asking the question, Where would a fence protect human life? One obvious answer is, around a swimming pool. Someone who builds a pool but fails to construct a fence around it should be held liable if a neighbor child wanders into the area and drowns.

These two examples illustrate how the Old Testament's general ethical principles continue to the present as guides to behavior that pleases God and protects us from harm and danger. The case laws retain their relevance by giving us ideas about how the general principles should be applied to a specific society. Developing the ability to move from general principles to specific situations is especially imperative in view of the massive changes that have occurred since Old Testament times. The people of God are no longer a nation, and the Messiah is no longer anticipated; he has come in the person of Jesus Christ. Accordingly, the application of the law has changed as well.

As we move from the Old to the New Testament, we note a fundamental difference in the nature of the people of God. In a phrase, the people of God in the Old Testament are a nation, a political body, but in the New Testament the people of God are a spiritual entity made up of individuals from many different nations. Israel as a nation was chosen by God. God had told them, "For you are a holy people, who belong to the LORD your God. Of all the people on earth, the LORD your God has chosen you to be his own special treasure" (Deut. 7:6). No other nation of the ancient or modern world matches Israel's place in redemptive history. Even if a majority of American citizens were sincere

Christians—or even if everyone were—America would not be like Israel in terms of God's redemptive history. In this connection it is significant to note that in the Book of Leviticus God presses obedience upon Israel because of their special status. Leviticus 11:45 is typical: "I, the LORD, am the one who brought you up from the land of Egypt to be your God. You must therefore be holy because I am holy."

In view of the foregoing considerations we must, before applying a case law or insisting on a penalty from the Old Testament today, take into account not only cultural adaptions, but also discontinuities attributable to Israel's unique status in redemptive history. How, for instance, would the difference in status between Israel and America change the laws that concern the divine-human relationship? Since God chose Israel as a nation to be his elect people, it was intolerable that a blasphemer or idolater or witch be allowed to live. God caused his special presence to rest in the midst of Israel; his holiness would not allow such blatant rebellion to continue. However, God has not chosen America as a nation. He does not dwell on the banks of the Potomac as he did on Mount Zion. It would be wrong to seek legislation authorizing the execution of witches, idolaters, apostates, heretics, and blasphemers in the United States or even to hope for a time when such legislation will be enacted.[19]

As has been traditionally recognized, the proper analogue to the nation of Israel is the Christian church. God chooses to make his special presence known in the assembly of the saints. He will tolerate no blasphemy, heresy, or idolatry in the midst of his priestly people. God has given spiritual weapons to his spiritual people to fight these spiritual enemies. Thus, instead of seeking the death of blasphemers the church proceeds with their excommunication.

God communicates his will for our lives through the Bible. The law of the Old Testament, with its explicit and direct demands on behavior, seems the most obvious place to go to discover what God desires in terms of behavior. Upon close examination, however, we have seen that it is not a simple thing to apply the Old Testament law and its penalties to the New Testament period. We must take into account not only cultural differences, but also redemptive-historical differences. The latter will have a definite impact on how the Old Testament civil laws, which have to do with the relationship between God and Israel, will be brought over into modern society. Each law and each penalty need to be studied in the light of the changes between Israel and America, the old covenant and the new covenant. Theonomy tends to grossly overemphasize continuity to the point of being virtually blind to the discontinuity. But we must be sensitive to the issues of discontinuity. Christians today are not a chosen nation in the period before the Messiah. Nonetheless, while wary of the extremes of theonomy, we must also keep in mind that the Old Testament law, when properly read in its canonical context, informs our understanding of God's will for our lives.

Obeying the Lord: Listening to the Whole Testament

There are two reasons why we have devoted considerable space to our discussion of the law in the Old Testament. In the first place, the law provides the most obvious answers to the question under consideration, namely, "How is the Christian to apply the Old Testament to life?" Imperatival in form, the law of God in the Old Testament intends to shape the lifestyle of the people of God in an obvious way. In the second place, while it is clear that God's intention in the law is to direct his people's life, the immediate recipients of the law were the Old Testament people of God, the Israelites. Thus it is not immediately clear, especially in view of apparent contradictions in New Testament references to the law, exactly how the Christian relates to the law today. Now that we have attempted to address that complex issue, it is time to press on. After all, the question at hand is how the Old Testament as a whole applies to our lives today.

God's Word as Seed and Mirror

Before looking at the various genres of the Old Testament, it will be well to briefly develop the idea that the Bible as a whole functions as a seed and a mirror in our lives.[20] The first metaphor is suggested by the parable of the sower, which Jesus told to a crowd by the lakeshore. Drawing from everyday experience, the story depicts a man flinging seeds out onto the ground. In those days of hand seeding, farmers would scatter the seeds in a wide arc on their small plots of land. Since the Galilean soil was fertile but extremely rocky, the seeds met different fates as they landed on different parts of the field:

> Some fell along the path, and the birds came and ate it up. Some fell on rocky places, where it did not have much soil. It sprang up quickly, because the soil was shallow. But when the sun came up, the plants were scorched, and they withered because they had no root. Other seed fell among thorns, which grew up and choked the plants, so that they did not bear grain. Still other seed fell on good soil. It came up, grew and produced a crop, multiplying thirty, sixty, or even a hundred times. [Mark 4:4–8 NIV]

Thus Jesus ended his story for the crowd on the shore, and they were left to contemplate what it all meant. However, when he withdrew with the small circle of his disciples, Jesus interpreted the parable. The seed is "the word," and the different fates of the seed correspond to the different ways people receive it:

> Some people are like seed along the path, where the word is sown. As soon as they hear it, Satan comes and takes away the word that was sown in them. Others, like seed sown on rocky places, hear the word and at once receive it with joy. But since they have no root, they last only a short time. When trouble or persecution comes because of the word, they quickly fall away. Still others, like seed sown among thorns, hear the word; but

the worries of this life, the deceitfulness of wealth and the desires for other things come in and choke the word, making it unfruitful. Others, like seed sown on good soil, hear the word, accept it, and produce a crop—thirty, sixty or even a hundred times what was sown. [Mark 4:15–20 NIV]

Most important for our purpose is Mark 4:14, "The farmer sows the word." Here Jesus identifies the seed with the gospel. The Word of God is a living seed that germinates in our souls and sends its roots down deep, transforming our whole being. Note that one of the essential qualities of the Word is that, like a seed, it is the agent of life. Some think of the Bible only as a book that prepares us for death. Yet the Bible is the place where we meet and develop a relationship with Jesus, who offers abundant life. Without Christ, life may have its short-term enjoyments and successes, but deep down we all know that there is as much pain in life as there is joy. The Bible equips us to deal with whatever life may bring.

A second essential quality is that the seed of the Word is a catalyst for growth. The Word is the place we go if we want to mature, to reach our fullest potential in all areas of our lives. If we earnestly read the Bible with an openness to its divine Author, it will change our minds, enrich our spirits, and guide us through each day. Nothing else is so powerful for change or so deeply fulfilling.

The Old Testament, as well as the New, can be an agent of change in our lives. Indeed, the Bible as a whole is the most powerful agent available today for transforming a life. Reading and studying the Old Testament in the context of the whole canon will transform each of us into someone truly beautiful.

Of course, if we are to change, we need to know who we are, and that is very difficult. Our hearts are so deceptive that we find it hard to know what is going on inside. We may struggle and not know the reasons why. Or we may be oblivious to the issues that hinder our growth in the Lord. Fortunately, God does not let us wallow in our ignorance. His Word reveals to us what is going on internally, the state of our soul.

Speaking of the invaluable role of the Word, John Calvin evokes the metaphor of a mirror: "What various and resplendent riches are contained in this treasure, it were difficult to find words to describe. . . . I have been wont to call this book, not inappropriately, an anatomy of all parts of the soul; for there is not an emotion of which anyone can be conscious that is not here represented as in a mirror."[21] We all know how a physical mirror works. Before leaving the house in the morning, we glance in the mirror to see if we are presentable. As a result, we may shave, comb our hair, straighten our tie. Calvin says that when we read the Bible, we get a close look at our inner selves and emotions, a gauge of our attitude toward God.

History: Lessons from the Past

We will keep the metaphors of seed and mirror in mind as we turn to the other major genres of the Old Testament to see how history, poetry, wisdom, and prophecy (including apocalyptic) intend, like law, to transform our lives. History is the predominant genre of the Old Testament. Starting with its first chapter and the creation of a formless mass that God shaped into the universe, it presents us with accounts of events that occurred in space and time. Genesis, Exodus, Leviticus, Numbers, Deuteronomy, Joshua, Judges, Ruth, 1 and 2 Samuel, 1 and 2 Kings, 1 and 2 Chronicles, Ezra, Nehemiah, Esther, and Jonah all purport to narrate space-time events. Even poetical books like Job tell a story that is set within a certain time period.

Today history is often wrongly thought to be a simple record of past events. Historians, however, are fully aware that it is impossible to report the facts of history apart from some kind of interpretive framework. Biblical history is no different. It does not simply register events; it provides an interpretive framework to guide our understanding of those events and to motivate us to a certain course of action. In this way, history becomes a stimulus to obedience toward God. As we recognize this function of biblical history, we become aware of our responsibility to apply the Old Testament to life.

As we study the history books of the Old Testament, it is important to view them as a theological history. In other words, the ideology that shaped them focused on God and his plan for the world. Thus the Old Testament presents us with a history of God's redemption of sinful humanity. This point is not to be confused with what German scholars of past generations meant by *Heilsgeschichte,* though that term can be legitimately translated "salvation history." *Heilsgeschichte* sometimes distinguishes between what the Bible reports as history and actual events. That is not our point. Our point is that all history is selective, shaped, and interpreted, and that the focus of Old Testament history is on what God is doing in the world, not on the political or military or economic forces in themselves. That history is presented from a certain interpretive perspective, namely, conviction that it is God who is moving the events of the world. For that reason biblical history is also called prophetic history; it was written by men who had received God's interpretation of history.

The theological nature of biblical historiography and the organic nature of God's plan for the salvation of his people explain why so much of the history anticipates the coming of Jesus Christ. Jesus is the center of that history because he brings to a climax the plan of God's salvation.

There is a school of thought that would stop at these crucial insights and say that they are not only the main, but the exclusive function of biblical history.[22] Specifically, members of this school rail against those who would take the Old Testament historical narratives and turn them into moral lessons: "Be courageous like Joshua!" "Don't be like Samson!" Unfortunately, it is true that much preaching on the Old Testament focuses on simple moral lessons and misses how the text under consideration elaborates on the great redemptive actions of God. Advocates of preaching that concentrates on redemptive history therefore do the church a great service by prodding preachers and teachers toward the bigger picture. However, as often happens in such situations, in their zeal to improve preaching they lose the benefits achieved through simple moral lessons. Their teaching and preaching are purely theological, and they look down on anyone who tries to teach a moral lesson from the Old Testament.

Paul himself would have us think otherwise. He is most clear on this in 1 Corinthians 10. Worried that the Corinthian church is being tempted to worship idols, he recalls an analogous situation in the past and applies it to the present:

> I don't want you to forget, dear brothers and sisters, what happened to our ancestors in the wilderness long ago. God guided all of them by sending a cloud that moved along ahead of them, and he brought them all safely through the waters of the sea on dry ground. As followers of Moses, they were all baptized in the cloud and the sea. And all of them ate the same miraculous food, and all of them drank the same miraculous water. For they all drank from the miraculous rock that traveled with them, and that rock was Christ. Yet after all this, God was not pleased with most of them, and he destroyed them in the wilderness. [1 Cor. 10:1–5]

Paul goes on to describe what the Israelites did to deserve destruction, and he warns the Corinthians to avoid similar behavior (vv. 6–11). A comment that bridges the hermeneutical horizons justifies Paul's application of Old Testament history to the Corinthian situation: "These events happened as a warning to us" (v. 6a).[23] In other words, part of the purpose of the record of the wilderness wanderings in Exodus through Deuteronomy is to serve as an object lesson for our behavior. These accounts are intended to keep us from pursuing idols, whether the stone and metal idols that tempted the Israelites and the Corinthians, or the less tangible idols of power, control, and wealth today.

However, we must be careful as we read the Old Testament and apply it to the present day. We have already had ample caution that there are both continuity and discontinuity between the two Testaments. Joshua's holy wars may not be used to justify contemporary wars, for there is no elect nation today. Some historical records do not portray normative behavior that God expects of all of his people all of the time. As we read the Old Testament for moral instruction, we have to ask ourselves whether the lesson still applies today. The best guide to answering this question is to see if the ethical teaching is presented in a more straightforward manner elsewhere in the Scripture, particularly in the New Testament.

Once again a brief look at Genesis 39, the story of Joseph and Potiphar's wife, will serve to illustrate. Clearly, the author presents Joseph as a paradigm of a virtuous young man. When his Egyptian master's wife invited Joseph to sleep with her (Gen. 39:7), he resisted by saying he would not betray his master or God (vv. 8–9). She then framed him, and he ended up in jail. Now this episode is extremely important in the history of redemption. After all, Joseph's meeting with the two Egyptian royal officials in jail propelled him and his dream-interpreting gift into the presence of the pharaoh and landed him in a position where he could care for his family during a horrible famine. And of course his family was not just any family, but the family of the promise. Joseph could later look back over his life and in response to his brothers say, "God turned into good what you meant for evil. He brought me to the high position I have today so I could save the lives of many people" (Gen. 50:20).

But as we study the story of Joseph in the framework of redemptive history, we should not lose sight of the fact that Joseph illustrates how a wise young man should act when tempted by sexual sin. This lesson is forcefully taught elsewhere in Scripture. By resisting Potiphar's wife, Joseph observes the seventh commandment, "Do not commit adultery" (Exod. 20:14). He also, at least from our later perspective, illustrates someone who has heard the advice of the sage in the Book of Proverbs to avoid immoral women (Prov. 5 and 7). Indeed, this connection is so strong that many have argued that Joseph is a historical incarnation of the wise young man of Proverbs.

Reading the Joseph narrative can empower us today to resist sexual temptation. Similar episodes in the various historical books of the Old Testament can have transformative power in our lives. In particular, they serve to shape Christian behavior by illustrating the blessings of obedience and making concrete the observe that the wages of sin is death.

Poetry: An Anatomy of the Soul

Poetry is the language of the heart, a mirror of our soul. It is the medium of love and intimate conversation. That is why it is the preferred style of the prophetic books and the prayers of Israel.

We will focus on the Psalms, the intimate prayers of Israel.[24] The psalmists share with God their most private feelings. They express the whole range of human emotion: joy, love, confidence on the one hand, and anger, shame, fear, contempt, jealousy, envy on the other.

While the Psalms were written in response to specific events in the lives of their composers (see, e.g., the so-called historical titles to Pss. 3 and 51), they were not written as historical records of these events. Rather, they are models of prayers for other worshipers who have had similar experiences. In this way, the Psalms are a mirror of our soul, articulating our own emotions better than we ourselves can.

Psalm 61 is a superlative example of a prayer that mirrors our own deepest feelings:

> O God, listen to my cry!
>   Hear my prayer!
> From the ends of the earth,
>   I will cry to you for help,

for my heart is overwhelmed.
Lead me to the towering rock of safety,
    for you are my safe refuge,
    a fortress where my enemies cannot reach me.
Let me live forever in your sanctuary,
    safe beneath the shelter of your wings!
For you have heard my vows, O God.
    You have given me an inheritance reserved for those who fear
      your name.

Add many years to the life of the king!
    May his years span the generations!
May he reign under God's protection forever.
    Appoint your unfailing love and faithfulness to watch over
      him.

Then I will always sing praises to your name
    as I fulfill my vows day after day.

The Bible describes the world as fallen (Gen. 3; Rom. 8:18–23), a fact that we, like the psalmist, know experientially as we encounter hostility and indifference on a daily basis. We long for the stability and safety that only God can provide. Psalm 61 puts into words our deepest feelings as the psalmist uses the images of a rock of safety and a mother bird to depict the sheltering comfort of God. By reminding us of God's protecting nature, the psalmist not only comforts us, but moves us so that we too will "always sing praises to your name" (v. 8).

Wisdom: Navigating Life in an Uncertain World

Wisdom in the Old Testament is a more profound concept than mere intelligence. To oversimplify, wisdom is more than a knowledge of facts; it is an ability to take those facts and make them work in the world. Wisdom is knowing how to do something, a skill. It is insight into navigating life on a daily basis.

There is a debate about the extent of the wisdom genre in the Old Testament, but everyone would agree to include Proverbs, Ecclesiastes, and Job in this literary-theological category. Today we identify biblical wisdom primarily with the pithy, practical sayings in Proverbs 10–31. These are short maxims that seem motivated by experience and common sense and, on the surface, easy to apply to life. The very first proverb is a good example: "A wise child brings joy to a father; a foolish child brings grief to a mother" (10:1). The obvious purpose of this observation is to motivate wise behavior, which is fleshed out in the proverbs that follow.

The proverbs often take on an imperitival form: "Teach your children to choose the right path, and when they are older, they will remain upon it" (22:6). When read in isolation, such proverbs seem similar to law, but not so clearly connected to theology. Indeed, the proverbs have often been characterized as secular or simply good advice. The book is then mined for practical insight into living.

However, such a viewpoint misleads in two crucial ways. First, it forgets that Proverbs is very clear about the religious foundation of a good life: "Fear of the LORD is the beginning of knowledge" (1:7). A careful reading of the first nine chapters of the book confronts the reader with a basic choice between a relationship with Lady Wisdom, who represents Yahweh himself, and one with Lady Folly, who represents a lifestyle that emanates from the worship of false gods.[25] Living life in the light of proverbial wisdom is more than a response to good advice; it is deeply theological. Wisdom is fearing God in our everyday actions. Here, then, is the most important lesson of the wisdom literature of the Old Testament. Being wise, at bottom, does not entail a mass of facts to be learned; it is a relationship with God. God is the repository of all wisdom (see Job 28 and 38–42). To become wise, human beings must turn to God.

The second common misconception is that proverbial wisdom, like moral law, is always and everywhere applicable to life. On the contrary, proverbs are context-sensitive. It takes a wise person to know when a particular proverb applies, to know when to speak a particular word: "Everyone enjoys a fitting reply; it is wonderful to say the right thing at the right time!" (15:23). Misapplication of proverbs is ridiculed in Proverbs 26:7 and 9: "In the mouth of a fool, a proverb becomes as limp as a paralyzed leg"; "A proverb in a fool's mouth is as dangerous as a thornbush brandished by a drunkard."

The context-sensitive nature of proverbs explains why we encounter seemingly contradictory advice in the book. This is nowhere illustrated more strikingly than in 26:4, 5:

> Do not answer a fool according to his folly,
> or you will be like him yourself.
> Answer a fool according to his folly,
> or he will be wise in his own eyes. [NIV]

In other words, the wise person will take the context into consideration and respond accordingly. That wisdom literature does not consist in laws but in context-sensitive principles does not lessen its relevance as we try to make our way through a difficult world. The purpose of wisdom literature is to give us principles for living and to shape our minds so we might be sensible in the application of those principles.

The books of Job and Ecclesiastes serve to restrain us from another common misconception about proverbial wisdom, namely, that a lifestyle of wisdom is a formula for success and prosperity. If one makes the mistake of reading the proverbs outside of their broader context, it is easy to fall into this error. Consider, for instance, the general principle enunciated in Proverbs 10:22: "The blessing of the LORD brings wealth, and he adds no trouble to it" (NIV). Yet Job was a wise man who suffered horribly. His three comforters believed that someone who truly follows God never experiences such misfortunes. Their conclusion was that

Job had to be a sinner, so their counsel was for Job to repent. But the first chapter of Job lets us in on the divine secret: Job is not suffering because of his sin.

The Teacher in the Book of Ecclesiastes affirms the utility of wisdom in navigating life:

> I saw that wisdom is better than folly,
>   just as light is better than darkness.
> The wise man has eyes in his head,
>   while the fool walks in the darkness. [Eccl. 2:13–14 NIV]

But note further that wisdom does not always mean a joyous and prosperous life:

> I have observed something else in this world of ours. The fastest runner doesn't always win the race, and the strongest warrior doesn't always win the battle. The wise are often poor, and the skillful are not necessarily wealthy. And those who are educated don't always lead successful lives. It is all decided by chance, by being at the right place at the right time. [9:11]

This truth depressed the composer of Psalm 73, a wisdom psalm. Having suffered, Asaph wondered about the usefulness of godly living, that is, until he adopted a long-range perspective. On earth it often appears that the foolish and evil person wins and prospers, while the godly suffer. In faith, however, the psalmist is assured that God's counsel is "leading me to a glorious destiny" (v. 24). Such truths of wisdom literature have shaped the lives of God's people through the ages and can offer much insight to Christians living at the dawn of the twenty-first century.

The Prophets: Warnings and Hope

From Abraham (Gen. 20:7) through Malachi prophets dot the landscape of Old Testament history. While their backgrounds and roles differed, they all served the purpose of communicating God's will to his people. What Moses, Isaiah, Nahum, Micah, and the others wrote had implications not only for their contemporaries, but also for us today.

We today tend to think that the prophets' chief role was to predict the future. And in fact God did reveal to many of them what would happen in the near as well as distant future. Since only the true God has such knowledge (Isa. 44:6–8), the prophet's predictive role naturally intrigues us. But study demonstrates that the prophets were only rarely interested in the future. Their message was directed to their contemporaries. They invoked the future either to console those suffering in the present or, more commonly, to call upon those sinning in the present to change their ways.

It is precisely in their role as harbingers of judgment that we see the ethical teaching of the prophets most clearly. Why did the prophets spend so much time chastising their audiences? The people of Israel had broken the covenant and the laws that God gave them after he entered into a relationship with them. He had warned them at the time that if they broke the law, they would be afflicted by the curses of the covenant. But before he activated those curses, he sent prophets to warn the people to change their ways before it was too late.

Given the nature of the covenant/treaty as a legal relationship, it is not surprising that the prophets often used legal language as they called their contemporaries to obedience. Micah 6:1–2 well illustrates this: "Listen to what the LORD is saying: 'Stand up and state your case against me. Let the mountains and hills be called to witness your complaints. And now, O mountains, listen to the LORD's complaint! He has a case against his people Israel! He will prosecute them to the full extent of the law.'" It is no wonder that the prophet in Israel has often been described as a covenant lawyer. He was sent by God to press his case against his disobedient people. The charges leveled against Israel were as broad as the law itself. They were sexually immoral, oppressive of the poor, exploitative, abusive, neglectful of religious obligations, murderous. At heart they rejected God. They broke all the commandments. The prophets' speeches of judgment were warnings to Israel and to us to follow the Lord closely.

So the prophets too are an important source of divine revelation telling us how to obey God. We should read them not just as a historical report, but as counsel on how to follow God more closely.

We began this chapter by asking the apparently simple question, "How is the Christian to apply the Old Testament to life?" We have seen that the answer is rich, but not easy. It is not simply a matter of putting ourselves in the position of the first audience and acting just as they did, for there are both continuity and discontinuity between the Testaments. Rather than discourage us, this truth should excite us to dive even more passionately and deeply into God's Word.

Notes

Chapter 1: "What Are the Keys to Understanding the Old Testament?"

1. Don Hudson, "Come, Bring Your Story," *Mars Hill* 1 (1994): 73–86.

2. For extensive information on biblical poetry see Tremper Longman III, "Biblical Poetry," in *A Complete Literary Guide to the Bible,* ed. Leland Ryken and Tremper Longman III (Grand Rapids: Zondervan, 1993), 80–94; idem, *Literary Approaches to Biblical Interpretation* (Grand Rapids: Zondervan, 1987), 119–50; idem, *How to Read the Psalms* (Downers Grove, Ill.: InterVarsity, 1988).

3. Quoted by Herbert Lockyer, "In Wonder of the Psalms," *Christianity Today,* 2 March 1984, 76.

4. Jeffrey J. Niehaus, *God at Sinai* (Grand Rapids: Zondervan, 1995).

5. For more information see John J. Bimson, *Redating the Exodus and Conquest* (Sheffield, Eng.: University of Sheffield Press, 1978).

6. For critical evaluation of contemporary scholarship on literary and hermeneutic theory, see Tremper Longman III, *Literary Approaches,* now reprinted in *Foundations of Contemporary Interpretation,* ed. Moisés Silva et al. (Grand Rapids: Zondervan, 1996); idem, "Literary Approaches and Interpretation," in *New International Dictionary of Old Testament Theology and Exegesis,* ed. Willem A. Van Gemeren, 5 vols. (Grand Rapids: Zondervan, 1997), 1:103–24; and idem, "Literary Approaches to Biblical Interpretation," in *The Face of Old Testament Study,* ed. David W. Baker and Bill T. Arnold (Grand Rapids: Baker, forthcoming).

7. For examples of Clines's approach to biblical interpretation see J. Cheryl Exum and David J. A. Clines, eds., *The New Literary Criticism and the Hebrew Bible* (Valley Forge, Pa.: Trinity Press International, 1993); and David J. A. Clines, *Interested Parties: The Ideology of Writers and Readers of the Hebrew Bible* (Sheffield, Eng.: Sheffield Academic Press, 1995).

8. The term "bespoke" indicates that the tailor makes clothes to order.

9. For his vegetarian reading of the Book of Job see David J. A. Clines, *Job 1–20* (Waco: Word, 1989), l–lii.

10. See Grant R. Osborne, *3 Crucial Questions about the Bible* (Grand Rapids: Baker, 1995), 11–71.

11. Walter C. Kaiser, Jr., *Toward an Exegetical Theology* (Grand Rapids: Baker, 1981).

12. For an annotated bibliography of some of the most widely used resources see Tremper Longman III, *Old Testament Commentary Survey*, 2d ed. (Grand Rapids: Baker, 1995).

13. See Longman, *Literary Approaches*, 76–83; D. Brent Sandy and Ronald L. Giese, Jr., eds., *Cracking Old Testament Codes: A Guide to Interpreting the Literary Genres of the Old Testament* (Nashville: Broadman and Holman, 1995); and Grant R. Osborne, *The Hermeneutical Spiral: A Comprehensive Introduction to Biblical Interpretation* (Downers Grove, Ill.: InterVarsity, 1991).

14. E.g., is the Song a drama or a psalter of love? For an excellent survey of the history of the interpretation of the Song, see Marvin H. Pope, *The Song of Songs* (Garden City, N.Y.: Doubleday, 1977), 89–229.

15. For such a use of the Song see Dan Allender and Tremper Longman III, *Intimate Allies* (Wheaton, Ill.: Tyndale, 1995).

16. For the arguments in favor of this identification along with a description of the genre and its use in the Bible, see Tremper Longman III, "Nahum," in *The Minor Prophets,* ed. Thomas E. McComiskey, 3 vols. (Grand Rapids: Baker, 1993), 2:771.

17. Ibid., 812.

18. See Richard J. Clifford, "The Use of *Hoy* in the Prophets," *Catholic Biblical Quarterly* 28 (1966): 458–64; Erhard Gerstenberger, "The Woe-Oracles of the Prophets," *Journal of Biblical Literature* 81 (1962): 249–63; Delbert R. Hillers, *"Hoy* and *Hoy*-Oracles: A Neglected Syntactic Aspect," in *The Word of the Lord Shall Go Forth: Essays in Honor of David Noel Freedman,* ed. Carol L. Meyers and M. O'Connor (Winona Lake, Ind.: Eisenbrauns, 1983), 185–88; Waldemar Janzen, *Mourning Cry and Woe Oracle,* Beiheft zur Zeitschrift für die alttestamentliche Wissenschaft 125 (New York: W. de Gruyter, 1972).

19. See Tremper Longman III, "Form Criticism, Recent Developments in Genre Analysis and the Evangelical," *Westminster Theological Journal* 47 (1985): 46–67.

20. For a fuller analysis see Tremper Longman III, "Psalm 98: A Divine Warrior Hymn," *Journal of the Evangelical Theological Society* 27 (1984): 267–74.

Chapter 2: "Is the God of the Old Testament also the God of the New Testament?"

1. See Dan Allender and Tremper Longman III, *Cry of the Soul* (Colorado Springs: NavPress, 1994).

2. O. Palmer Robertson, *The Christ of the Covenants* (Grand Rapids: Baker, 1980); and Walter C. Kaiser, Jr., *Toward an Old Testament Theology* (Grand Rapids: Zondervan, 1978).

3. Elmer A. Martens, *God's Design* (Grand Rapids: Baker, 1981).

4. See Meredith G. Kline's attempts in *The Structure of Biblical Authority* (Grand Rapids: Eerdmans, 1972).

5. There is a heated debate over the status of the covenant idea before the time of Noah. Some Reformed scholars maintain that even though the word does not appear before Genesis 6:18, the covenant concept is operative right from the begin-

ning of the biblical record and is an appropriate description of the relationship between God and Adam and Eve even before the fall.

6. For English translations of these ancient Near Eastern treaties see *Ancient Near Eastern Texts Relating to the Old Testament,* ed. James B. Pritchard, 3d ed. (Princeton: Princeton University Press, 1969), 199–206, 531–41.

7. Note, e.g., the so-called royal psalms (Pss. 47, 93, 96, 98, 99, 100) that celebrate God's kingship.

8. Robertson, *Christ of the Covenants,* 271.

9. Ibid., 276.

10. For a detailed presentation of this theme see Tremper Longman III and Daniel G. Reid, *God Is a Warrior* (Grand Rapids: Zondervan, 1995).

11. See Marten H. Woudstra, *The Ark of the Covenant from Conquest to Kingship* (Philadelphia: Presbyterian and Reformed, 1965).

12. See Yigael Yadin, *The Art of Warfare in Biblical Lands* (New York: McGraw-Hill, 1963).

13. For more on ḥerem-warfare see Longman and Reid, *God Is a Warrior,* 46–47.

14. Indeed, there are psalms that were composed in a prebattle context (Ps. 7), a battle context (Ps. 91), and a postbattle context. See Tremper Longman III, "Psalm 98: A Divine Warrior Victory Psalm," *Journal of the Evangelical Theological Society* 27 (1984): 267–74.

15. W. L. Moran, "The End of the Unholy War and the Anti-Exodus," *Biblica* 44 (1963): 333–42.

16. For this period of time see Lester L. Grabbe, *Judaism from Cyrus to Hadrian* (Minneapolis: Augsburg Fortress, 1992), vol. 1.

17. Tremper Longman III, *Literary Approaches to Biblical Interpretation* (Grand Rapids: Zondervan, 1987), 88–91.

18. This point is debated by Gordon J. Wenham, *Genesis 1–15* (Waco: Word, 1987), 62–64.

19. Genesis 4:4–5 most likely implies, though it does not explicitly mention, an altar.

20. In the early part of the narrative Abraham goes by the name Abram. For the sake of consistency we will refer to him by his later, longer name throughout.

21. We are not making the case that every altar was built near a tree; the text does not allow us to press our point that far. On the other hand, the association occurs too frequently to be mere coincidence.

22. Moriah could have been an earlier name, or perhaps the name of a ridge on which Zion was a prominent peak.

23. The interruptive passage also explains why the Levites were given priestly status.

24. For an example of an allegorical reading of the tabernacle narratives see Paul F. Kiene, *The Tabernacle of God in the Wilderness of Sinai* (Grand Rapids: Zondervan, 1977).

25. Carol L. Meyers, *The Tabernacle Menorah* (Missoula, Mont.: Scholars, 1976).

26. Longman and Reid, *God Is a Warrior,* 64.

27. See Tomoo Ishida, *The Royal Dynasties in Ancient Israel* (New York: W. de Gruyter, 1977).

28. Because Chronicles was written while the second temple was being built during the postexilic period, it is intensely concerned with the construction of the first temple. See Roddy L. Braun, *1 Chronicles* (Waco: Word, 1986), xxix–xxxii.

Chapter 3: "How Is the Christian to Apply the Old Testament to Life?"

1. "Jot and tittle," the smallest marks in the Hebrew writing system, is a literal translation of "smallest commandment."

2. See Bruce K. Waltke, "Theonomy in Relationship to Dispensationalist and Covenant Theologies," in *Theonomy: A Reformed Critique,* ed. William S. Barker and W. Robert Godfrey (Grand Rapids: Zondervan, 1990), 58–86.

3. That there is variation within dispensationalism is indicated by the rise of the movement called progressive dispensationalism; see Darrell L. Bock and Craig A. Blaising, *Progressive Dispensationalism* (Wheaton, Ill.: Victor, 1993).

4. C. I. Scofield, *Rightly Dividing the Word of Truth* (Findlay, Ohio: Fundamental Truth, 1940), 5.

5. Waltke, "Theonomy," 60.

6. See in particular the masterful, but ultimately misguided work of Greg L. Bahnsen, *Theonomy in Christian Ethics* (Nutley, N.J.: Presbyterian and Reformed, 1977). Among other significant theonomic thinkers are Rousas J. Rushdoony and Gary North.

7. In flagrant disregard of Acts 15, Rousas J. Rushdoony, *The Institutes of Biblical Law* (Nutley, N.J.: Presbyterian and Reformed, 1973), goes as far as to advocate that Christians keep kosher.

8. Perhaps the best-known study help is the Scofield Reference Bible.

9. DeMille was the director and producer of the movie *The Ten Commandments,* which was made in 1956 and starred Charleton Heston and Yul Brynner.

10. For an excellent contemporary exposition see J. Douma, *The Ten Commandments: Manual for the Christian Life,* trans. N. D. Kloosterman (Phillipsburg, N.J.: Presbyterian and Reformed, 1996).

11. Perhaps the best-known law collection from the ancient Near East outside of the Bible is the Code of Hammurabi (c. 1700 B.C.); other collections include the Laws of Ur-Nammu (2100 B.C.) and the Lipit-Ishtar Lawcode (c. 1850 B.C.). For translations of these and other Mesopotamian laws, see *Ancient Near Eastern Texts,* ed. James B. Pritchard (Princeton: Princeton University Press, 1969), 159–98, 523–30.

12. Richard E. Averbeck, "Law," in *Cracking Old Testament Codes: A Guide to Interpreting the Literary Genres of the Old Testament,* ed. D. Brent Sandy and Ronald L. Giese, Jr. (Nashville: Broadman and Holman, 1995), 120.

13. For a fuller discussion see Tremper Longman III, "God's Law and Mosaic Punishment Today," in *Theonomy,* ed. Barker and Godfrey, 40–54.

14. Bahnsen, *Theonomy,* 445. We have excluded the Scripture references that Bahnsen provides, since they are not disputed. What is disputed is their continuing validity.

15. Rushdoony, *Institutes*, 235.

16. Rousas J. Rushdoony, *Law and Society* (Vallecito, Calif.: Ross House, 1982), 699–700.

17. Rushdoony, *Institutes*, 231.

18. Walter C. Kaiser, Jr., *Toward Old Testament Ethics* (Grand Rapids: Zondervan, 1983), 127–37. Kaiser's work is based in the main on Stephen A. Kaufman, "The Structure of the Deuteronomic Law," *Maarav* 1 (1978–79): 105–58.

19. Contra Greg L. Bahnsen, *By This Standard* (Tyler, Tex.: Institute for Christian Economics, 1985), 152; idem, *Theonomy*, 445, 540; Rushdoony, *Institutes*, 38.

20. See Tremper Longman III, *Reading the Bible with Heart and Mind* (Colorado Springs: NavPress, 1997).

21. See Tremper Longman III, *How to Read the Psalms* (Downers Grove, Ill.: Inter-Varsity, 1988), 13.

22. For a description of the debate see Sidney Greidanus, *Sola Scriptura: Problems and Principles in Preaching Historical Texts* (Toronto: Wedge, 1970).

23. In this case the NIV is more precise to the Greek and more to the point: "These things occurred as examples to keep us from setting our hearts on evil things as they did."

24. For more on the Psalms see Longman, *How to Read the Psalms;* and Dan Allender and Tremper Longman III, *Cry of the Soul* (Colorado Springs: NavPress, 1994).

25. The culmination is found in Proverbs 9, where Lady Wisdom and Lady Folly both appeal to the reader to enter an intimate relationship. The reader can choose only one! For more detail see Longman, *Reading the Bible,* 155–58.

Recommended Reading

Allender, Dan, and Tremper Longman III. *Bold Love.* Colorado Springs: Nav-Press, 1992.

———. *The Cry of the Soul.* Colorado Springs: NavPress, 1994.

———. *Intimate Allies.* Wheaton, Ill.: Tyndale, 1995.

Baker, David W., and Bill T. Arnold, eds. *The Face of Old Testament Study.* Grand Rapids: Baker, forthcoming.

Dillard, Raymond B., and Tremper Longman III. *An Introduction to the Old Testament.* Grand Rapids: Zondervan, 1994.

Kline, Meredith G. *The Structure of Biblical Authority.* Grand Rapids: Eerdmans, 1972.

Long, V. Philips. *The Art of Biblical History.* Grand Rapids: Zondervan, 1994.

Longman, Tremper, III. *How to Read the Psalms.* Downers Grove, Ill.: Inter-Varsity, 1988.

———. *Old Testament Commentary Survey.* 2d ed. Grand Rapids: Baker, 1995.

———. *Reading the Bible with Heart and Mind.* Colorado Springs: NavPress, 1997.

———, and Daniel G. Reid. *God Is a Warrior.* Grand Rapids: Zondervan, 1995.

Martens, Elmer A. *God's Design.* Grand Rapids: Baker, 1981.

Osborne, Grant R. *The Hermeneutical Spiral: A Comprehensive Introduction to Biblical Interpretation.* Downers Grove, Ill.: InterVarsity, 1991.

Robertson, O. Palmer. *The Christ of the Covenants.* Grand Rapids: Baker, 1980.

Ryken, Leland, and Tremper Longman III, eds. *A Complete Literary Guide to the Bible.* Grand Rapids: Zondervan, 1993.

Sandy, D. Brent, and Ronald L. Giese, Jr., eds. *Cracking Old Testament Codes: A Guide to Interpreting the Literary Genres of the Old Testament.* Nashville: Broadman and Holman, 1995.

Scripture Index

Subject Index

Tremper Longman III (Ph.D., Yale University) is professor of Old Testament at Westmont College and one of evangelicalism's leading biblical scholars. He has written numerous works on both scholarly and popular themes, including *The Book of Ecclesiastes, How to Read the Psalms,* and *Literary Approaches to Biblical Interpretation.*